D1096318

KEN

It is with a dreadful sense of shock that we record
the death of our friend and colleague
Ken Purdy, who died by his own hand on the morning
of June 7th, 1972. He was fifty-nine.
To us, Ken was one of the most interesting men alive,
an incomparable companion and the best
automotive writer who ever lived. He is irreplaceable.

We offer our deepest sympathy to Ken's dear wife Lucy,
and to his son and daughter, Geoffrey and Tabitha.
Our own loss, though not as great as theirs, is deeply felt.

automobile
Quarterly

THE CONNOISSEUR'S MAGAZINE OF MOTORING TODAY, YESTERDAY AND TOMORROW

Third Quarter 1972   *Volume X, Number 3*

LIMITED EDITION

PUBLISHER AND PRESIDENT:
L. SCOTT BAILEY

EDITOR:
DON VORDERMAN

MANAGING EDITOR:
BEVERLY RAE KIMES

ASSOCIATE EDITOR:
RICHARD M. LANGWORTH

ART DIRECTOR:
THEODORE R. F. HALL

ASSISTANT ART DIRECTOR:
KENNETH N. DRASSER

EDITORIAL ASSISTANT:
ROBERTA SCHOTTLAND

CHIEF OF RESEARCH:
HENRY AUSTIN CLARK, JR.

RESEARCH ASSOCIATES:
JAMES J. BRADLEY, LESLIE R. HENRY, U.S.A.
MICHAEL SEDGWICK, GREAT BRITAIN
GIANNI ROGLIATTI, ITALY
NICOLAS FRANCO, JR., SPAIN

CONTRIBUTING EDITORS:
WILLIAM BODDY, RUSS CATLIN,
MAURICE D. HENDRY,
KARL E. LUDVIGSEN, DENNIS MAY,
JAN P. NORBYE, DAVID OWEN,
ROBERT F. SCOTT, CARL L. WAGNER

ARTISTS:
THOMAS E. FORNANDER, WALTER GOTSCHKE,
JOHN HANNA, PETER HELCK, JOHN PECKHAM,
YOSHIHIRO INOMOTO, TED LODIGENSKY,
LESLIE SAALBURG, DALE WEAVER TOTTEN

PHOTOGRAPHERS:
HORST H. BAUMANN, GIORGIO BELLIA,
STANLEY ROSENTHALL, JULIUS WEITMANN

PRODUCTION MANAGER:
CHESTER R. DETURK

CIRCULATION MANAGER:
JOHN HEFFELFINGER

BUSINESS MANAGER:
JACOB R. ESSER

AUTOMOBILE *Quarterly* IS PUBLISHED QUARTERLY BY AUTOMOBILE *Quarterly*, INC., EDITORIAL OFFICES: 40 EAST 49TH STREET, NEW YORK, N. Y. 10017. TELEPHONE: PLAZA 8-2374. OFFICE OF PUBLICATION: 245 WEST MAIN STREET, KUTZTOWN, PENNSYLVANIA 19530. TELEPHONE: 683-7341. AUTOMOBILE *Quarterly* IS PRINTED IN THE UNITED STATES BY THE KUTZTOWN PUBLISHING COMPANY ON AUTOMOBILE *Quarterly* ENAMEL, A SPECIAL PAPER PRODUCED BY THE S. D. WARREN COMPANY, NEW YORK CITY; COLOR SEPARATIONS BY LITHO-ART, INC., NEW YORK CITY; BINDING BY NATIONAL PUBLISHING COMPANY, PHILADELPHIA, PENNSYLVANIA. SINGLE COPIES: $6.95; ANNUAL SUBSCRIPTIONS: $24.50 IN U. S., $25.50 ELSEWHERE. ALL SUBSCRIPTIONS, ORDERS, CHANGES OF ADDRESS AND CORRESPONDENCE CONCERNING SUBSCRIPTIONS SHOULD BE SENT TO 245 WEST MAIN STREET, KUTZTOWN, PENNSYLVANIA 19530. SECOND-CLASS POSTAGE PAID AT KUTZTOWN, PENNSYLVANIA AND AT ADDITIONAL MAILING OFFICES.

© AUTOMOBILE *Quarterly*, INC. 1972. ALL RIGHTS RESERVED UNDER PAN AMERICAN AND UNIVERSAL COPYRIGHT CONVENTIONS BY AUTOMOBILE *Quarterly*, INC. REPRODUCTION WITHOUT PERMISSION IS PROHIBITED. LIBRARY OF CONGRESS CATALOG CARD NUMBER 62-4005.

CONTENTS

STUDE

One Car
a
Remem
in Sou

by
Maurice

"By corporate bylaw, three men decided on the product — the chairman of the board, the president and the chairman of the finance committee. And as my good friend R. A. Vail, vice-president of production, said, at the end, 'It didn't seem to make any difference who was president. Every time they came to a fork in the road they always took the wrong turn'." Such was the comment, in retrospect, of a highly regarded engineer who served Studebaker Corporation for more than forty years.

In March of 1966 the company no longer had the problem of choosing which fork to take — they were already at the end of the road. In the bitterness of the plant's shutdown Vail's comment is understandable, but it doesn't do credit to the positive side of the record. Studebaker had been in transportation a long time. Behind them stretched a one-hundred-fifteen-year trail of horse-drawn and horseless vehicles built for virtually every purpose and distributed to every part of the globe, from Norway to New Zealand, from Brazil to Zanzibar. Most automobile manufacturers could claim they had helped their country in two world wars. Only one could say that it had supplied vehicles for the military needs of both General Ridgeway and Secretary of War Stanton.

Although the Studebaker name persists today within a corporation now active in other fields, those activities need not be of concern in these pages, but rather Studebaker's century-plus in transportation, focusing on the automobile years. The Studebaker wagon-building era — longer in duration, but less expansive in scope — provides the prelude, and in the ensuing years of the marque lent to it an unmistakable aura of grass roots Americana.

The founder of the Studebaker dynasty in America was Peter Studebaker, who came from Holland with his family aboard the good ship *Harle* in 1736. The Studebakers landed at Philadelphia, settled in Pennsylvania and in the years following established themselves as wood workers and blacksmiths. A tax list of 1798-99 from the then Huntingdon Township, York County, notes one Peter Studebaker, Sr. and Peter Studebaker, Jr. as wagonmakers. The latter's son John followed the same trade and started his own business a dozen miles north of Gettysburg, where an historic marker still indicates the foundations of his works. Anticipating the famous Horace Greeley dictum, John Studebaker subsequently went west — to Ohio — in 1835. Naturally he travelled in one of his own wagons, the traditional Conestoga type, an example of which is still preserved in the Studebaker Historical Collection in South Bend, Indiana.

John's five sons — Henry, Clement, John M., Peter E. and Jacob F. Studebaker — grew up to look like portraits from the pages of *True West*, which their actual careers did not belie. Most "Western" of them all was John

BAKER

Do Lot of ... ering ... th Bend

... Hendry

M., who in 1853, at the age of nineteen, fell victim to gold fever and left for California in a wagon train. The year previous, on February 16th, 1852, Henry and Clem had pushed west too, establishing the firm of H. & C. Studebaker, blacksmiths and wagon builders, in South Bend, Indiana. Their equipment consisted of two forges, and their capital totaled sixty-eight dollars. They built two or three wagons in 1852 and made some painful progress over the years that followed. In 1856 they built their first carriage. But they were still struggling, and in need of more capital.

Meanwhile John M. had been earning good money in California — not mining nuggets but in meeting miners' transportation requirements. The nature of these can be guessed from his nickname: "Wheelbarrow Johnny." After five years he had amassed, if not a fortune, a worthwhile bank balance, and his brothers in South Bend prevailed upon him to return and inject their company with fresh capital. With $8000 John M. bought out Henry's interest and invested in the company. Henry thereafter took up farming, but later Peter E. joined the now burgeoning firm, taking charge of sales. Branch houses were soon established in Salt Lake City, San Francisco and Portland, Oregon. The firm became an important supplier to the U.S. Government during the Civil War, and by 1868 annual sales had reached $350,000.

That year the brothers formed a corporation, The Studebaker Brothers Manufacturing Company, with Clem as president, John M. vice-president, Peter E. treasurer and Jacob F. secretary. Four years later their literature advertised: "The Largest Vehicle Builders in the World — Facilities Sufficient to Make a Wagon Every Seven Minutes." Growth continued through the Nineties, annual sales passed two million dollars and dealers were established in foreign countries. Studebaker vehicles attained a fine reputation with British military forces in the Boer War; Lord Roberts reported to Parliament that Studebaker wagons "proved superior to any other make, either of Cape or English manufacture."

Inevitably, with the advent of the horseless carriage, the company interested itself in this new mode of transport. John M. wrote on August 6th, 1895, that, "In reference to the gasoline engine now being manufactured by the Worth Manufacturing Company of Benton Harbor, Michigan. We had already considered the possibility of adapting it to a vehicle, and we are giving the subject of horseless carriages very careful attention. At the present time our own Mr. Fish has this matter in charge."

In the spring of 1897 the minutes of the directors recorded experiments with a "horseless vehicle." By 1899 the company was building bodies for electric runabouts manufactured elsewhere. In 1902 Fred Fish (Studebaker's cor-

Conestoga
wagon, 1850's

Phaeton, 1857

THE GREAT
CARRIAGE & WAGON FACTORY
At South Bend, Indiana.

STUDEBAKER BROS.

The Arrangements for 1867 and 1868 are Complete.

Founded in 1852 with willing hands and stout hearts, but no capital. We have struggled upward, overcoming all discouragements, until to-day we employ

One Hundred and Thirty Hands,

And turn out MORE WORK than any other Wagon Factory in Indiana. We are willing to abide by the injunction "by their works ye shall know them." Let our works praise us; we ask no other indorsement. We claim to be

Unsurpassed in excellence of Workmanship and Material, And we make our prices such that no prudent man will claim to undersell us. On this base we plant our flag, and here we propose to fight to the end. Confident of our ability we declare to all men that we will not surrender while a "shot remains in the locker," nor while we have the means to justify our proposed end, which we assert to be

ENTIRE AND UNCONDITIONAL SUCCESS.

Our reputation, our interests, "all we are and all hope to be," are involved in making good our pledges, and all we ask is that the public will give us a trial. If we are able, as we know we are, to maintain ourselves agains all opposition, we will vindicate our motto,
"LABOR OMNIA VINCIT."

Our stock is complete and perfect. Wagons, Carriages, Buggies, Sleighs, and all vehicles always on hand in great variety, or made to order with dispatch.

WORK FULLY WARRANTED.
STUDEBAKER BROTHERS.

poration lawyer, a director and son-in-law of John M.) persuaded the rest of the board to build some electric runabouts of their own, designed by Thomas Alva Edison. The first of twenty built that year went to a Mr. R. W. Blees of Macon, Missouri, on February 12th. John M. himself used one to drive around the plant, up ramps onto the roof and across the bridges between buildings.

Late in 1903 Fish brought two engineers named McMasters and Dennison into the company. Although John M. Studebaker was not at all impressed by gasoline automobiles, which he described as "clumsy, dangerous, noisy brutes" which "stink to high heaven, break down at the worst possible moment and are a public nuisance," he was persuaded by Fred Fish to give grudging blessing — and the first gasoline-powered Studebaker left the factory on July 22nd, 1904. It was all very carefully stage managed. Fred Fish drove the car out into the street where, as factory workers cheered, news reporters took notes and photographers clicked their cameras, he was stopped by a man who asked the price of the car. Told it was $1250, the man discovered he just happened to have that sum on his person, handed it over and took possession of the car on the spot. The buyer was H. D. Johnson, another son-in-law of John M. Studebaker.

The car was a two-cylinder model of 16 hp, whose chassis was supplied by the Garford Company of Elyria, Ohio, with body and final assembly by Studebaker. It had the usual "American-type" construction of the day: central engine position, horizontally mounted under the floor, chain drive and dummy hood. Bore and stroke measured 5 x 5½ inches, for a displacement of 209 cubic inches. The five-passenger touring car was priced at $1250, with the top a $150 extra.

In 1905 a front-engined four-cylinder shaft-drive model of 20 hp appeared, priced at $3000, and a series of fours were built up to 1908 in collaboration with Garford. The directors soon saw that cars at this price could never sell in quantities commensurate with their existing position in the vehicle industry and sufficient to employ the facilities of the plant and world-wide sales organization. The answer lay in "moderately priced automobiles that could be built and sold in large quantities." In September of 1908, therefore, the company obtained exclusive rights to the sale of cars built by a new company just emerging in Detroit: the Everett-Metzger-Flanders Company, organized in March that year by Barney F. Everett, a large-scale accessories manufacturer, William E. Metzger, former sales manager of Cadillac, and Walter E. Flanders, ex-manufacturing manager of Ford Motor Company. Their advertising manager was E. Le Roy Pelletier, formerly Ford's advertising manager. The chief

Surrey, turn of the century

Factory, early 1900's

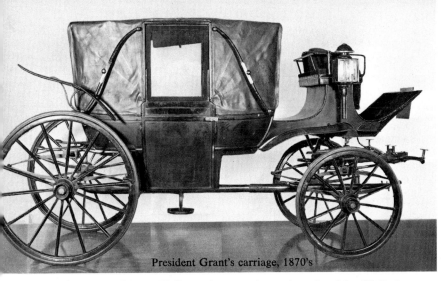

President Grant's carriage, 1870's

engineer was Thomas Walburn, the general superintendent Max Wollering.

The firm bought the plants of Northern and Wayne as well as the early Ford plant on Piquette Avenue in Detroit. Two hundred Wayne cars were built during the first part of the year — and the E-M-F 30 was designed, tooled and built in 172 units before the end of the year. Designated A-30, the four-cylinder (4 x 4½) car was priced at around $1000 and was notable for its lack of a water pump, relying on thermo-syphon cooling. Unfortunately the engines overheated with uncompromising regularity, so the factory recalled all 172 cars and installed water pumps, this addition becoming a standard item on all cars following. While the majority of sales in 1908 had been Studebaker-Garfords, the situation was reversed in 1909 when 7960 E-M-F's were made. In January of 1910 the Flanders model S-20 was introduced with a 3⅝ x 3¾ engine, and 15,364 cars were manufactured. The Garford was phased out, although its chief consulting engineer, Hayden Eames, came into Studebaker where he eventually rose to general manager. That same year Studebaker bought control of E-M-F.

In 1911 a total of 27,653 Flanders 20's and E-M-F 30's were built, and on February 14th that year the Studebaker Corporation was organized, representing the assets of Studebaker Brothers and E-M-F. The financing was handled

Studebaker-bodied electric, 1899

by the banking firms of Goldman Sachs and Company and Lehmann Brothers of New York. John M. Studebaker was chairman, Fred Fish president, Clem Studebaker, Jr. first vice-president, George M. Studebaker vice-president and A. R. Erskine treasurer.

During 1912 the previous year's models were continued in production, 29,123 cars being built. And Studebaker chief engineer James G. Heaslet designed two new four-cylinder cars: model SA-25 (3½ x 5) and model AA35 (4⅛ x 5), which were introduced in December that year. Henceforward all cars would be Studebaker-designed. Already decided, in August, was the fact that they would bear the name Studebaker, the E-M-F and Garford designations being dropped, although for a time manufacture of the former Flanders 20 and the E-M-F 30 were continued.

There were several reasons favoring Studebaker as a brand name. Everett and Metzger had left about 1910 or 1911 to attempt — the word is used advisedly — revival of their names in new automobile concerns, and Flanders made a similar try early in 1912. Garford was no longer of any account, and Studebaker now controlled the whole enterprise. However, the probable main reason for name changing was a purely practical one. Like many contemporaries, the E-M-F had been designed with transmission on the rear axle. In those days of noisy gears, this made for a quieter car — one reason Packard used it — but it naturally resulted in a heavy axle. In a commendable attempt at lightness, the E-M-F used a cast aluminum combination differential and transmission housing. But there were many field failures and the E-M-F was labelled (or libelled) with the classic indictments of "Every Morning Fixit" and "Every Mechanical Failure" — and, best of all, "Easy Mark's Favorite."

A former Studebaker engineer recalls that "the almost continual rear axle failures and the epithets applied to the product by the public threw the organization into near panic and much confusion prevailed. You can readily imagine the backlash which followed. They tested everything, and 'for life'. . . as a result of all this frenzied testing a series of really rugged cars later emerged . . . [the] famous Big and Special Sixes."

But we are getting ahead of our story. The first step after discarding the name was to get rid of the trouble itself. On the two new cars introduced late in 1912 the rear axle was redesigned using a pressed steel banjo housing for the differential and replacing the aluminum casting with an iron one, still retaining the transaxle principle. Studebaker made all the parts except the pressed steel banjo which was supplied by Timken. This design changed markedly improved the axle, and although the cast iron carrier increased the assembly weight, the pressed steel axle housing was light. Another notable early application of this material was on the 1913 models which had one-piece drawn fenders. These were made by the Pressed Steel Sanitary Manufacturing Company of Detroit, which Studebaker had bought in 1911. This concern had some of the largest deep drawing presses in the industry — up until then they had been making bathtubs.

Another important advancement appearing on the 1913 six-cylinder models was the monobloc engine casting, certainly one of the first and, it appears, shared with only one other make — Premier — that year. The 1913 line of six different models was rationalized down to two only for 1914: a four and a six with similar engine dimensions (3½ x 5). This change was tied into a reorganization of production for economy, and continued as a policy until after World War I.

Studebaker's engineering division evolved from the E-M-F organization. An engineering laboratory had been set up during 1911 by chief engineer James G. Heaslet and his assistant Fred M. Zeder. It was enlarged as the focus of Studebaker research in 1913, and when Heaslet became vice-president of

Frederick S. Fish

Albert Russel Erskine

1904 Model C
Owner: B. Rademacher

President Taft
in 1904 touring car

J. M. Studebaker
seated at left
in early electric

Pittsburgh showroom,
circa 1905

Electric of 1908
used in Senate-
to-House subway,
Washington, D.C.

1906 Model F-28
Harrah's Automobile Collection

1909 E-M-F 30
Owner: M.T. Studebaker

1912 Flanders 20
Owner: F. Robinson

engineering, Zeder was appointed chief engineer. Heaslet had been associated with automobiles since 1897, back when Studebaker first began experimentation. He was typical of the early engineers whose credentials were vague and who were really little more than competent mechanics. Lacking theoretical background, they relied on mechanical savvy, which many of them had in far greater degree than trainees fresh from college.

Zeder represented the first of a new crop — university graduate engineers, the forerunners of the technologists of today. He earned a B.S. in mechanical engineering at the University of Michigan in 1909 and worked at Allis Chalmers before coming to Studebaker E-M-F. Aged twenty-eight in 1914, he was reputedly the youngest chief engineer in the business. He was shortly joined by two other graduate engineers: Owen R. Skelton, who had worked at Pope-Toledo and Packard, and Carl Breer, who had met Zeder at Allis Chalmers. A brilliant triumvirate, their harmonious combination of talents would earn for them the sobriquet "The Three Musketeers."

Heaslet resigned as vice-president in the spring of 1917 (although continuing on the company's payroll until July, 1918) and took charge of airplane production and inspection in Detroit for the Aircraft Production Board. Later, in the Twenties, he became president of Rollin. He was succeeded as engineering vice-president by Max F. Wollering, a thirty-eight-year-old Wisconsin-born toolmaker who had extensive experience at Allis Chalmers, International Harvester, Ferro Machine and had also come into Studebaker via E-M-F.

In July of 1915 Fred Fish retired from Studebaker presidency and became chairman of the board. He was succeeded by Albert Russel Erskine, who had been first vice-president from December, 1913, and who had in fact been running the company from that date. John M. Studebaker remained listed in company literature as "Honorary President," but the title was as meaningless as it sounds. The directors might call him "J.M.," a few others might address him as "Mr. Studebaker," but the vast majority simply stared at him on his occasional visits to the plant, wondering who the devil he was. As a legend he was formidable, but he had never been a force of any consequence in Studebaker's entry into the automobile field: That had been the work of Fish, whom Erskine himself described as a man of "foresight, initiative and effort."

Now it was Erskine's foresight, initiative and effort that were given full rein. He had originally come in as "a hatchet man for the banks." At first sight of him the natural reaction was to ask what W. C. Fields was doing in an administration post. He was a somewhat ruthless, overbearing and ill-mannered man who gained plenty of enemies. He could be vindictive and make capricious decisions, solely on personal feelings. One such incident, involving the termination of Studebaker's entire advertising account with one agency and its granting to another, arose from a dispute over a game of poker!

Nevertheless, allowing all these debits, it has to be admitted that Erskine was extremely capable and probably the most dynamic leader the company ever had. His promotion had been gained on merit, and the record of Studebaker under him for many years showed that his judgment was well founded. Starting with finances and ranging through all fields to workers' welfare, he had an excellent grasp of the requirements for running a large corporation. This was true through most of his two-decade tenure.

Erskine's first four months in 1911 as treasurer were typical of his methods. He took no office, sat at no desk. He moved from department to department, investigating, learning, analyzing and reorganizing. Wasteful duplication was eliminated and unnecessary or incompetent staff dismissed. Costs were cut and accounting centralized.

During World War I Studebaker first supplied the Allies, then devoted its resources entirely to Uncle Sam. But in May, 1917, Erskine directed the

1913 Model 35AA
Owner: Louis R. Mahnic

engineering staff to start preparing for postwar conditions. Immediately Zeder, Skelton and Breer, assisted by consulting engineers, began work on three new cars. Three experimental models were built and on September 15th — just four months after management's instruction to start — the cars were secretly pushed aboard a boat at Detroit and quietly rolled off at Buffalo, where Erskine joined the engineers for the test. The cars were driven through Canada and the U.S. for 20,000 miles. Tests were carried out at Saranac Lake, New York, with financiers present. "A chapter could be written about the results," says one industry salesman. "These tests opened the minds of several groups of auto builders of that day." (Among them, it would appear, was the directorate of Studebaker itself. Despite the strong backbone that Zeder-Skelton-Breer constituted, management remained unsure of the engineering department, a hangover perhaps from E-M-F days. As a second string, in 1917, they asked consultant Alanson P. Brush to prepare alternative designs. These were never necessary, but it is amusing that the plans remained in South Bend's engineering files until cessation of vehicle production there in 1964, when they were finally destroyed.)

In December the three Zeder-designed cars were put on the Chicago speedway where they completed a further 30,000 miles driven day and night,

The formidable "Granddaddy"

The Blish brothers and proud father, in tourer the boys drove 3000 vacation miles from Indiana to New England and back, 1913

Test driver on daily run from No. 1 plant, Detroit

with thirty mechanics and engineers in attendance. Limited production began that month for the 1918 model year, two cars — the Light Four Model SH and the Light Six Model EH — being all new, and the Big Six being revised in the light of test data. A major change was the moving of the transmission from the axle up to the engine. One Big Six tourer built in 1918 covered 500,000 miles as a test car in the ensuing five and a half years. Its test crew named it "Granddaddy."

Studebaker had once tried to do without a water pump and failed. In the Teens they tried to do without another item of the cooling system. Zeder designed an aluminum head that was simply a lid, i.e. it had no water passages although manifold passage was cast integral. Cooling was satisfactory but the aluminum of the day was too porous for a good compresssion seal. The chemists evolved a satisfactory vacuum-impregnated bakelite varnish cure, but this interesting experiment was abandoned after several thousand Light Sixes had been built.

In 1919 Studebaker broadened the use of pressed steel, from rear axle housings to oil pans and many other components, reducing both cost and weight. For 1920 they dropped the four-cylinder and introduced a new Light Six as its replacement, while the former Light Six, now improved, became a Special Six,

so that there was a line of three sixes, the Light, the Special and the Big Six. On arrival in England one of the new models was tried by A. C. F. Hillstead, sales manager for Bentley, who commented: "That motorcar was certainly a good performer, being extremely quiet and possessed of excellent top gear acceleration."

All models shared cast en bloc L-head six-cylinder engines. Rated at 23, 29 and 36 hp, they developed an actual 40, 50 and 60 bhp respectively. They were not outstanding for efficiency, but conversely, their inbuilt durability and toughness gained them great renown under world-wide conditions. Statistics show that sales of replacement parts in 1921 were twelve percent lower than in 1919, despite 118,000 new cars sold in that period. In 1921 the sale of parts averaged $16.00 per car. In 1924 it had fallen to $10.84. To quote an apt comment by Erskine: "These are the cars that made Studebaker famous."

In 1920 Zeder, Skelton and Breer left to set up as consultants and later became the nucleus of Chrysler engineering. Guy P. Henry now became chief engineer of Studebaker. He maintained an "all six" policy during his six-year tenure, playing it safe, doing exactly what Erskine told him and seemingly leaving no particular mark, compared with what had gone before and what was to come later. However, his regime can be credited with the introduction of

World War I tractor for Britain, 1918

Company military band, 1925
Inset: leader
M. P. Kelly

"Spirit of Spring" promotion for the 1928 President

Eighteen-foot-high President replica at Proving Ground 1930 to 1936

molybdenum steel — contemporary with (some claim earlier than) Wills Sainte Claire. At the same time the aluminum cone clutch formerly used gave way to a single dry plate clutch designed and built by Studebaker. In September of 1924, for the 1925 model year, the Duplex Phaeton was introduced, with a hard-top and glass rear quarters. During 1925, too, the Light Six became known as the Standard Six.

An interesting but short-lived interlude (1925-26) was the hydraulic servo braking system, consisting of a transmission-driven oil pump which operated a mechanical brake linkage by hydraulic pressure. It came with four wheel brakes, and operated on both front and rear wheels, with a mechanical override on rear wheels only. This was because the power unit was ineffective below 15 mph or in reverse. (It was also a reserve system in case of servo failure.)

"The brake pedal had two zones of operation," recalls a Studebaker engineer. "The first two inches of movement controlled the power brake, but if the pedal was depressed over two inches the rear mechanically-operated brakes only were in effect. . . . No great imagination is required to guess what happened when a panic stop was made. I can testify to [having had] some rather startling moments behind the wheel."

Henry was responsible to engineering and manufacturing vice-president Max Wollering. Assisting Henry were consulting engineers Vincent Link and E. J.

Miles, chief body engineer J. H. Bourgon, methods and standards manager W. P. Woodside and two men, Leroy Maurer and A. J. Chanter, who would later head engineering and administration at Pierce-Arrow.

Studebaker's plant facilities were enormous, having been continuously expanded since 1914. By the mid-Twenties the original vehicle plant in South Bend had been relegated to small forgings, stamping springs and certain body parts manufacture. Separate buildings for Light, Special and Big Six models were added in 1922-23, these alone totalling well over one million square feet of floor space. At capacity, a total of 5200 bodies were in process at any one time, a complete body taking from nineteen to twenty-one days to complete.

All chassis components for Light Sixes were made at South Bend's Plant 2, which included an extensive and up-to-the-minute foundry opened in 1924. Its floor area was 575,000 square feet and its capacity 600 tons of castings daily. As a result of their engineering testing, Studebaker insisted on steel companies supplying steel alloys to their own specifications. Use was also made of alloys in the cast iron mix, and here they could do as they chose because they had their own foundry. Plant 3, at Detroit, made complete chassis for Special Six and Big Six models, and had over three-quarter million square feet of floor space. Plant 5, also in Detroit, was the service parts store and shipping facility, and also housed the executive offices of the manufacturing, engineering, ex-

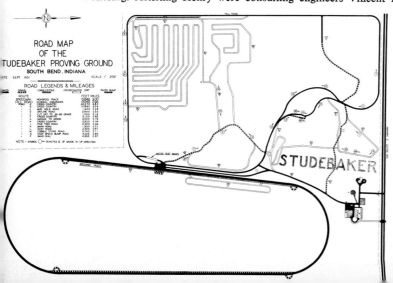

Barney Roos

perimental and methods and standards departments. Plant 7, in Walkerville, Canada, assembled Detroit, South Bend and some Canadian components into complete cars for Canadian and British Empire trade. By siting it there the cars could be advertised as "British built" and qualify for reduced tariff.

Altogether, the total plant area covered 225 acres with buildings occupying seven and a half million square feet of floor space. Annual production capacity was 180,000 cars, requiring 23,000 employees. A pointer to the vast postwar expansion lies in the fact that of the $50,000,000 plant value, $39,000,000 or seventy-eight percent had been added since November, 1918.

Studebaker's aim, like Ford, was to become more competitive by eliminating the profits of middlemen. Hence the extensive plants, the foundry, and the body shops. Factory literature pointed out that although a quarter of the cost of a car lay in its engine and a third in the body, few makers had their own foundry and fewer still their own body plant.

Exports were now important and the corporation maintained an extensive dealer and sales force around the world. Studebaker, Hudson and Buick dominated global markets in their price range in the same way as the Model T, the Chevrolet and the Dodge did in theirs — this despite frantic efforts by English and European car-producing countries: horsepower tax, import duties, appeals to patriotism and nonsensical propaganda against "Woolworth quality" cars. Erskine himself commented that although "there are upward of 150 automobile producers in England and 125 in France, not one possesses facilities equal to those of the leading United States manufacturers. . . . When European manufacturers compete with American cars in agricultural and non-automobile producing countries they are unable to make much headway." Even in Britain, France, Italy and Germany, he continued, "American cars are sold in fairly large quantities, despite high tariffs."

Erskine visited Europe in 1924. He gathered a mass of data about European trends, inspected Continental factories and called Studebaker's European dealers together for a meeting in Paris. Each dealer was asked to give his specific recommendation as to the ideal car for European use. Out of that conference, held October 10th in the Restaurant Langer, there arose a new car with a new name and of new concept.

For a name they selected Erskine's own, and took advantage of both the low taxation and fuel costs of the cheap European car and the smoothness, comfort and style of the larger American car. The idea had already arrived in the shape of the Essex, but Studebaker slyly got in a dig at its somewhat pedestrian reputation by advertising the Erskine as "The Little Aristocrat." They bolstered this claim by instancing its attractive styling —"expressive of the genius of R. H. Dietrich, recognized as one of the world's leading designers of custom bodies." The poor little Essex, on the other hand, was still living down its "packing crate" appearance, and could not claim any connection with the elite.

The Erskine's small bore engine (2⅝ x 4½ for a 146-cubic-inch displacement) gave a low European taxation at 16.54 rated hp, but developed 40 at 3200 rpm on the brake. Early ads claimed "60 mph with safety, 25-30 miles per gallon, 5 to 25 mph in eight and half seconds, 11% grade on high gear," a remarkable combination considering the roomy body. And it was all achieved on a 107-inch wheelbase.

The car was heralded by impressive publicity, both at home and abroad, when announced in October of 1926. The French dubbed it "Le Clou du Salon"; from London's Olympia came orders for over 2000 cars taken during the show alone, plus comment such as "Greatest auto value in British History — How can they do it?" Back in Detroit, company literature told of exhaustive testing at the "Million Dollar" Studebaker Proving Ground (opened that year) when Ralph De Palma and company engineers had selected it from

1923 Special Six
Owner: Phil Reed

fifteen models after extreme trials. And there was frequent mention of Dietrich.

However, the recollections of one Studebaker engineer are more to the point: "The recurring impossible dream! All companies tried the low-price field — Ford was not the only one, though until Chevrolet he was the only successful one. Studebaker was no exception. The many times they tried were with the Flanders, the SA-25 of 1913, the SF of 1916, the Light Six of 1920, the Erskine, the Rockne Six of 1931, the Champion of 1939 and the Lark of 1959."

"The Erskine was in the nature of an experiment, rather a half-hearted one at that. It was to feel out the sales potential and was based on a very meager investment. The car was an assembled one, Continental making the engine, and all other parts or components being purchased from stock. The body was specially tooled, but otherwise all parts were stock. The car was badly overpriced at $995, because in 1927 Ford brought out the Model A for $525. . . . The Erskine had poor engine life, because to overcome the low torque, a high numerical axle ratio (5.125) was used. Likewise, production life was mercifully short, ending in 1930."

Meanwhile a new man had come to work at Studebaker. Guy P. Henry had never moved to South Bend, and in 1926 he left the company to take up the development of an oil burner in Pennsylvania. He was killed a year or two later in an explosion, while experimenting. Henry's successor was Delmar G. Roos,

1923 Light Six
Owner: E. J. Uzumecki

1926 Big Six
Owner: Richard LaBree

better known as "Barney" because of his youthful admiration for Barney Oldfield. The nickname suited, for he was almost as colorful as his hero and, like him, never at a loss for words.

"Barney Roos was one of the most articulate men I have ever met in my life," one associate twinkled. "If I ever saw anyone who could talk and prove a point and know what he was talking about, it was Barney. He could tell you more in five minutes than most people could tell you in an hour." Even the autocratic Erskine was taken aback. Accustomed to having the engineering staff under his thumb, with no back answers from any of them, including Henry, Erskine had once said that "the engineers are just there to take orders from the sales guys." But Roos was too strong to be dominated. "He just overwhelmed Erskine," a contemporary remembers with a grin. It was a new experience for the company president, but to his credit, he recognized Roos' worth and the two men got along well.

Barney was born in the Bronx, New York, in 1888. After attending Manual Training High School in Brooklyn, he studied engineering at Cornell, earning degrees in the mechanical and electrical courses. He also distinguished himself as a photographer (one picture he took of a three-horse fire engine team was syndicated throughout the world) and as an athlete (winning the intercollegiate and national fencing championships). A brilliant conversationalist on art,

drama, economics, politics and science, he was tall, well built and handsome, despite somewhat protruding teeth. He left a great impression on the Studebaker staff. "He was an original thinker, and a tremendous doer," recalls one. "I think I never saw the man unless he was on a dead run."

On graduating from Cornell in 1911 Barney had joined General Electric, where he worked under Dr. Sanford Moss on steam, gas turbine and centrifugal compressor development. A year later he went to Locomobile as assistant research engineer. In 1919 he was assistant to Pierce-Arrow's David Fergusson, and followed the latter briefly as chief engineer in 1921. He then returned to Locomobile, where he succeeded Andrew L. Riker as chief engineer. In 1925 there was an interlude as chief at Marmon. Then he came to Studebaker.

His first task was the removal of the entire engineering department and personnel from Detroit to South Bend and installation of both in a new building. During this confusion Barney also managed to redesign the Standard Six and Big Six engines, make many changes in the chassis and oversee the redesign of the bodies.

One engineer who still has vivid memories of Roos at this juncture is Clyde R. Paton. Paton himself has had a distinguished career of over a half century in automotive, aeronautical and allied fields. He came to Studebaker in October of 1925, having been hired in Detroit by research chief Leon Chaminade and was subsequently one of nine men — whose number included also John A. C. Warner, John Sly and Harold White — whom W. S. James took with him to South Bend to set up a research center. "Barney!" Paton recalls. "He was a prima donna, par excellence! He had endless temperament and he used me as his safety valve. The engineering department was a two-story building with the experimental garages on the ground floor. We were on the first floor, and my office was at the top of the stairs. Barney never seemed to make the turn past my office to his own. He blew his top at me in my office every morning when he came in! It didn't make any difference whether he was going for me or someone else. Five minutes after he stormed out, the phone would ring. It would be Barney, asking me to come in. He'd simmered down and it was all over. Actually I nominally reported to Bill James, but occasionally Barney got other ideas. . . . Barney Roos was bombastic, a gay liver, had a tremendous vocabulary and a brilliant mind. He was an extremely capable engineer and, except when he gave me hell, I thought he was swell."

Barney's counterpart in body engineering was J. V. Hughes, who had succeeded J. H. Bourgon as chief body engineer. "Like Barney, Jimmy Hughes was highly opinionated — and had the ability to express himself beautifully," chuckled Paton. "I recall one visit he made to the experimental section where we were working on bodies and using scientific methods to diagnose body vibration, compare the inherent damping qualities of wood versus steel bodies (we found the latter had none) and so on. All this was quite new to Jimmy, of course. I remember his comment still. He said, 'Mr. Paton, a body is just a comfortable enclosure for passengers. Nothing more.' Of course, when he and Barney disagreed the fireworks were something to see and hear. What a pair they made!"

Barney's greatest contribution at Studebaker was in changing the exhaust note. Under his regime — and very soon — the song of the Big Six gave way to the silken purring of eight cylinders in line. Roos was already an authority on straight eights, having designed the Locomobile Junior Eight and the Marmon Little Eight. Neither of these were exactly triumphs of engineering, but they gave him a considerable basis of experience from which the soundly-based Studebaker straight eights emerged.

The first of these was the 1928 President Eight, announced January that year. It had an L-head five main bearing engine with integral cast block and

1927 Standard Six
Owner: William Cannon

1927 Erskine Deluxe Model 50
Owner: Samuel Alcorn

1927 Erskine Model 50
Owner: Becky Stitt

crankcase. Bore and stroke were 3⅜ x 4⅜ (312.5 cubic inches) with a power output of 100 bhp at 2600 rpm. The five-passenger sedan, with a wheelbase of 131 inches, weighed 4000 pounds and was priced at $1985.

The President Eight was joined in the 1928 model year by the Commander Six and the Dictator Six. The former had a 3⅞ x 5 engine of 354 cubic inches developing 75 bhp at 2400 rpm. Its wheelbase was 120 inches, and the five-passenger sedan weighed 3560 pounds and was priced at $1495. The Dictator had a 3⅜ x 4½ bore and stroke, 242 cubic inches and 67 bhp at 2700 rpm. The five-passenger sedan, with a wheelbase of 113 inches and weight of 3260 pounds, carried a price tag of $1245.

Accompanying these cars was the President Six, on a 127-inch wheelbase and powered by the hairy 354-cubic-inch engine. Introduced in 1927, it was available in a 1928 only as long as it took to sell off the remaining copies.

Of these four cars and three engines, the President Eight had the best horsepower-to-weight ratio. The Commander had the best displacement-to-weight ratio and so much torque that it carried only a 3.31 axle, while the others employed 4.08 or more. The three sixes were in concept the lineal descendants of a lineup that had been introduced around the end of the world war. They were loaded with torque in the driving range typical of the early Twenties but short of breath at the higher speeds now coming into vogue. That

favorite label —"rugged"— had described them well. But with roads improving there was less need to overdesign for extreme conditions. Consequently the new Roos eights were more efficient in output per cubic inch, more lithe in appearance and feel, livelier and more responsive, smoother and quieter, and more refined in general.

For 1929 the Commander remained at 75 hp (now from 248 cubic inches) and the President Eight — originally designated FA — continued to metamorphose. Its 313-cubic-inch engine had been increased to 337 (115 hp at 3200 rpm) in mid-1928 and introduced, too, had been a shorter 121-inch wheelbase FB model. In January of 1929 the new models were termed FE (135-inch wheelbase) and FH (125-inch wheelbase). Noteworthy features were the Bendix mechanical brakes, mechanical fuel pump and ball-bearing spring shackles. The model names introduced in 1927, President, Dictator and Commander (there was a Chancellor in 1927 too, but that year only) would serve Studebaker well.

The smaller bore eight-cylinder principle moved down to the Commander line in January, 1929, when the 3 1/16 x 4¼, 250.4-cubic-inch Commander Eight was announced. It developed 80 bhp at 3600 rpm. For two years it shared its 120-inch wheelbase chassis with the Commander Six, the latter being dropped after 1930. The Dictator series received the same treatment when in June

1929 President
Owner: Richard L. Saddler

of 1929 the Dictator Eight (3 1/16 x 3¾, 221 cubic inches, 70 bhp at 3200 rpm) appeared. For a year it was accompanied by the old Dictator Six.

The President Eight, as a road machine, had few equals in its price class or above it. The Speedway special had a 7:1 cylinder head, a special carburetor with larger throat and main jet and a high lift cam giving 165 hp. With the standard 3.47 axle, the car was guaranteed to do 90 mph.

In 1931 Cliff Bergere drove a President Eight out the Garst Street gate at the back of the engineering building, having punched the time clock at eight in the morning. He returned as the clock was striking noon that same day. He had gone for a little jaunt to Indianapolis, 150 miles away, had driven round Monument Circle and returned, having covered the 300 miles at an average speed of 75.25 mph. "Of course, it was depression times," recalls one engineer. "Nobody cared what speed you drove; there were no stoplights operating, and Cliff pretty much had the road to himself. He could drive wide open wherever the road permitted. Even so, remembering the road conditions forty years ago, it was some performance. The car was completely stock. . . ."

"The President Eight was really a go-getter," the engineer continued. "I personally owned one, the first model, a 1928 five-passenger opera coupé with very light body. I drove it back and forth to work. At the time of the 1932 Indianapolis race trials when Studebaker entered a team, the boys in the engineering department were playing round with the '32 race cars and they made many sets of special high compression heads and rear axle gears. When they were through with the '32 race they offered a bunch of that stuff for sale through the salvage. I bought a hi-com head which was painted red and a 2.94 rear axle ratio specially cut for the race cars. I put this in the coupé. Being young and foolish in those days, I had lots of fun because this old coupé was then five or six years old and worth about fifty bucks in the dealers' books. Nobody suspected that it had any performance. New car drivers were always thunderstruck when they were operating at top speed on the highway — say eighty miles an hour or so — and this old coupé would go flashing by with me at the wheel. . . . Incidentally, I got real good economy with the 2.94 axle. As I recall it used to get around fifteen to the gallon."

The interesting thing about the two smaller straight eights was the use of *nine* main bearings instead of five as in the "father engine," the President. Later, in July of 1930, this feature was introduced on the President itself. Why this was done is unknown, but it may have resulted from the association of Studebaker and Pierce-Arrow engineering that started in 1928 when South Bend gained control of the Buffalo firm. The two engineering departments remained as separate entities throughout the five-year liaison, but during this period there was a constant interchange of staff, ideas, designs and practices — and both organizations worked toward standardization with the aim of reducing costs and avoiding duplication. Among Studebaker engineers who went to Buffalo were Karl M. Wise, Leroy Maurer, Arthur Chanter and Maurice Thorne.

The Pierce-Arrow straight eight featured nine main bearings from inception. Both it and the Commander Eight had been announced in January, 1929, but the semi-fusion of Studebaker and Pierce-Arrow engineering had begun in August of the previous year. Thus, despite the common belief that the straight-eight Pierce was influenced by Studebaker, it is more likely that the eight-cylinder Studebakers of the Thirties reflected Pierce-Arrow thinking — an instance of fable upside-down from fact.

In the case of another Roos engine design of this period, fact was even stranger than fable. Having produced several straight eights, Barney proceeded a step further: During 1931 he designed, built and tested an inline *ten*-cylinder engine. The likely reasons for this oddity were that it was an alternative to the Pierce twelve then under development, might have been simpler, and made use

1929 President
Formerly A. N. Rodway collection

of existing straight-eight experience. It had six main bearings with a crankshaft designed along six-cylinder lines. After many failures a one-piece cylinder head was superseded by one in two sections with the exhaust manifolds also in sections, each having an expansion joint. The test engine was installed in a long wheelbase, seven-passenger sedan, and test drivers familiar with eights, twelves and sixteens acclaimed the ten as the smoothest they had ever driven. The project was dropped because of the likely production costs, impractibility of such extreme length and no doubt the successful advent of the Pierce-Arrow twelve.

Another idea Roos took up with gusto at this time was free-wheeling. He and W. S. James presented a paper on it to the SAE after it had been adopted on Studebakers in July of 1930. Company advertising billed it as the greatest advancement since the self-starter. Actually it was neither a new idea, nor of much real benefit with standard transmission, because synchromesh (now making its appearance) gave easy shifting without loss of engine braking. Free-wheeling was quickly taken up by many other makes — and just as quickly dropped. But it later proved an invaluable adjunct to automatic overdrives, in which form it survives today. Although dismissed as a gimmick in its initial form, free-wheeling as developed by Studebaker and Warner Gear Company eventually proved to be a worthwhile contribution.

1931 Series 54
Owner: William Wecker

1930 Commander
Owner: William Cannon

Probably the most notable advancement of this period was hidden down in the engine where few people other than engineers and service mechanics ever noticed it. It derived from aero-engine practice. To overcome bearing failures in Liberty engines they were converting to various uses, Allison in Indianapolis (later a division of General Motors) had originated the high capacity, coated-steel shell bearing for crankshafts. In collaboration with Cleveland Graphite Bronze Company (now Clevite Corporation), Studebaker developed this bearing for automobiles and introduced it in production in 1931. More than any other feature, this is responsible for the lower-end stamina of the high speed engine today.

The substantial technical progress Studebaker was making reflected the solid corporate foundation established by Erskine and the confident engineering department inspired and directed by Roos. Few independent companies were so powerful technically. In fact the only companies who had proving grounds in the modern sense at this time were General Motors, Studebaker and Packard, who opened their facilities in 1924, 1926 and 1928 respectively. In contrast Ford and even Chrysler lacked extensive proving grounds until after World War II.

"Full credit for Studebaker's early start must go to Erskine," recalls one company engineer. "He saw the need — unlike Henry Ford, who never did — and authorized the expenditure. Of course, I think he realized it had good publicity value as well, and to this end, along the north boundary a big grove of trees was planted. Seen from the air, they spelled the word STUDEBAKER clearly even at ten thousand feet." (They still do though the present owners of the proving grounds would no doubt prefer them to spell BENDIX.)

Laid out by ex-GM engineer Maurice Thorne, who had earlier supervised construction of the gigantic GM facility at Milford, the Studebaker proving grounds covered 840 acres and had a banked three-mile oval for sustained high speed tests. For breakdown endurance tests, there was a road of blacktop and gravel "built so ingeniously rough that a thousand miles at forty or fifty mph is worse than 9000 or 10,000 miles of normal driving," claimed a company booklet. "Ditches are cut diagonally across some stretches. High chassis-twisting mounds alternate on right and left. There are special roads where the car or truck stirs up terrific dust or must fight its way through deep sand, grades of 30%, 45% and 60%, and a waterhole detour where the driver must plunge through a 250 foot concrete basin. Sometimes the water is mixed with sand or cinders depending on what the engineers are trying to find out about the car's ability to 'take it'."

1931 President "Four-Season"   Owner: William A. Spencer

1931 President "Four-Season"
Owner: Bob Foust

Vehicles tested fell into four categories: new Studebakers under development, production models taken at random from the line as a check, domestic competitors and European cars, the last named being selected only in case of significant styling or engineering advancements.

The "recurring impossible dream" recurred again in 1932, only a couple of years after the Erskine's end. The Rockne must be the only car ever named after a gridiron coach. Kenneth "Knute" Rockne was a national institution. He was killed in a plane crash early in 1931, and apparently neither the good fathers of South Bend's University of Notre Dame, nor the Rockne family, had any objections to Studebaker's use of his name for a new Studebaker light car to supersede the Erskine. (The idea had been discussed with Coach Rockne before his untimely death and received his approval.) So in February of 1932 the Rockne Six was announced. It was priced much lower than the Erskine ever had been, some models were under $600 and none reached $800. It had an L-head six-cylinder engine in two sizes: 3⅛ and 3¼ x 4⅛, 190 and 205 cubic inches, delivering 66 and 72 bhp at 3200 rpm. There were two wheelbases, 110 and 114 inches, and two standard final drive ratios, 4.55 and 4.73. The five-passenger sedans weighed 2675 and 3000 pounds.

In specifications and appearance the Rockne resembled the contemporary Plymouth Six introduced in 1933. But although it appeared a year earlier, the Rockne attained only a tiny fraction of the Plymouth's sales. Only 23,201 were built and it was phased out in 1933. In October that year all former Rockne cars were registered as Studebaker-Rocknes. Like the Erskine the Rockne failed to give the buyer anything he couldn't already get from the well-established Big Three: Chevrolet, Ford and Plymouth. Moreover, Ford in 1932 had introduced a V-8 which outperformed and undersold the Rockne just as the Model A had the Erskine. And while the A had two cylinders less than the Erskine, the V-8 had two cylinders more than the Rockne.

Still, the Rockne was a better car mechanically than the Erskine had been. "Contrary to its predecessor," says one former Studebaker engineer, "the Rockne was a very well designed little car. It had a new engine — Studebaker designed and built, and known as the model A. It was continued, after the Rockne was withdrawn, in the Dictator Six of 1934-35-36-37 (stroked to 4⅜ inches in 1936) and eventually became a truck engine. [To point out just how good a design it really was, it appeared later in the 1938 Model 7A Six, as well as in Commanders from 1938-1942 and both Commanders and Land Cruisers from 1947-1950.] It was made until the machinery was finally scrapped about 1961. It had the longest run of any engine of any six-cylinder car I ever heard of — over thirty years — and we wore out so many sets of patterns in the foundry that I can't remember how many runs were used. Incidentally, one of the main reasons it was discontinued for trucks was that the foundry patterns had worn out for the umpteenth time, and the expense of making a new set was too high to justify continuing the engine. . . . I was the fellow who originally set up the Rockne plant in Detroit — did all the dickering, buying, layouts and got it rolling. Then I returned to South Bend. And it was Bert Fowler and myself with a gang of men and fourteen trucks who over Easter weekend 1933 closed down the Rockne plant and transferred everything to South Bend. There it was integrated into the Studebaker line."

The end of the Rockne coincided with the demise of the man whose name the Rockne's predecessor had borne. Albert Russel Erskine in 1933 was no longer the driving, dominant, ruthless and confident man of a few years earlier. Now he was sick, disillusioned — and beaten. His sickness was serious: heart trouble and diabetes. His disillusionment came from the repeated failures of his efforts to bolster Studebaker stock by operating as though the Depression had never happened. In 1930 he had declared a dividend of $7,800,000, which was

five times the actual net profits of that year. In 1931 he paid out nearly three million dollars in dividends — not from profits but from capital. By the end of 1932 Studebaker's working capital had been reduced to $3,500,000. Liabilities exceeded assets by fifteen million dollars. When the banks called the Studebaker loans, the company could not pay. Erskine had hoped to retrieve the situation by a merger with White, who had been cautious from the start of the Depression and had substantial cash reserves. When a minority of White stockholders blocked the deal, Erskine was confident that he could bludgeon them into acceptance, but when he appeared at a meeting in New York to decide the issue, instead of small-time stockholders he found himself facing the representatives of the Chase Manhattan Bank. Erskine returned to South Bend a defeated and broken man.

In March of 1933, unable to meet six million dollars in bank loans, Studebaker went into receivership. Harold Vance, Paul Hoffman and Ashton G. Bean, the latter chairman of the board at White, were put in charge of Studebaker affairs. Erskine moved his office out to his home on the outskirts of South Bend. Apart from the corporation's disaster he also faced personal bankruptcy. Three months later he found a simple but drastic solution to his problem, dying by his own hand. According to one account, the insurance companies duly and promptly paid all his debts and provided for his dependents.

1932 President
Owner: Willis O. Johnson

1932 Dictator St. Regis Brougham
Owner: Dick Osbourne

Providing for Studebaker's future took longer. There had been a two-week shutdown of the production line in March. Early April saw it move again, and that month the sale of Pierce-Arrow stock brought in a million dollars cash. By the end of April the reformed Studebaker Corporation was actually showing a profit — even if it was only twenty thousand dollars — and in 1934 Hoffman obtained nearly seven million dollars from bankers. By 1935 the company was again healthy, with Hoffman as president and Vance board chairman.

Paul G. Hoffman had once been an auto salesman and had more recently built up a prosperous Studebaker distributorship in Los Angeles. In 1925 he had joined the corporation in South Bend as vice-president of sales. Vance had risen successively within a period of twelve years from a mechanic in the factory to head of specifications, purchasing agent, assistant to the president, foreign sales manager and sales manager. In 1926 he succeeded Max F. Wollering as vice-president in charge of engineering and production.

Under these two the company made a creditable recovery, although never to regain the position held in the Twenties during which Studebaker loomed a while as a possible third part of a Big Three (a position ultimately taken by Chrysler). But the extent of the revival can be gauged by the fact that from receivership in 1933 Studebaker proceeded within a few years to the point where management could again take one of their compulsive cracks at the low-priced market. First, however, we should review engineering changes — technical and personnel — during the mid-Thirties.

The big 337-inch President Eight had been dropped after 1933. Continued were a low-priced six (under $1000) using the Rockne-based engine with various strokes and known diversely as the Studebaker Six, the Dictator Six and the Special Dictator Six. Concurrently, there were the two eight-cylinder models, the Commander and the President. The former had a 221-inch engine of 103 hp and a wheelbase of 119 inches. It was priced from $940 to $1165. The President had a stroked version (4½ inches) of the Commander Eight engine, giving 250 cubic inches and 110 bhp at 3600 rpm. It had a wheelbase of 123 inches and was priced from $1170 (or five dollars above the dearest Commander) up to $1420.

Probably the most notable features were the beaver-tail styling of the 1934-35 Land Cruiser models, inspired by the rakish Pierce Silver Arrow (the bodies for which had actually been built at Studebaker), the "planar" independent front suspension introduced on 1935 models and the Warner overdrive adopted the same year. None of Studebaker's rivals outside of GM and Chrysler could claim true independent front suspension, except Packard. (The Baker system used by Nash and Hudson was only semi-independent.) Studebaker's planar system, designed by Barney Roos, was very successful and was used for a con-

1932 Rockne Model 65
Owner: Wally Olson

1937 President by Salmons & Sons
Owner: Rolf C...

1939 President
Owner: Sheldon Henderson

Paul G. Hoffman

siderable period. It anchored a large transverse leaf spring to the frame, aided by upper and lower links, the upper being tubular to absorb brake torque. The first series had Houdaille rotary shock absorbers connected to the steering knuckle by a linkage, the second, introduced in 1937, used direct-acting telescopic units made by Delco. The transverse leaf spring was used because its inherent friction damping avoided the need for an anti-roll bar.

Noteworthy for 1936 was the Hill Holder, that coupling between clutch pedal operation and master cylinder of the hydraulic brake system which eliminated backward rolls on uphill stops. (Press brake and clutch, remove foot from brake, press accelerator, release clutch — the hydraulic pressure created by original press of the brake was thus released and the car moved forward . . . or more literally, upward.)

Other features keeping Studebaker abreast or ahead of medium-priced competition were vacuum power brakes and automatic choke, while certain not-so-obvious engineering details were advanced enough to be "discovered" as late as the Sixties and trumpeted by other makers. Instances were the celeron spoke cam gear (for which development the company received a Modern Plastic plaque in recognition), Hancock rotary door latches and, in 1937, variable ratio steering giving a 19.5 ratio straight ahead (for faster response) and a

24:1 at the sides (for easier parking). Incidentally, the latter idea was originally used by Alanson Brush on the 1910 Brush runabout, so even Studebaker could not claim it as a first.

In engine design great strides had been made in a few years. Whereas in the Twenties bearing failure was certain at a continuous 3800 rpm, by the Thirties Studebaker engines were capable of 100 hours at 4000 rpm, full load, full throttle. In fact, from 1937, the engine durability requirement was fifty hours at 4000, plus fifty hours at 4500. At the latter speed the 1937 engine showed far less wear than a 1929 engine run only at 3800 rpm. Studebaker attributed this to their "first" — steel-backed bearings, plus lighter alloy pistons. They acknowledged the lightness of bored-out crankshafts, but avoided them because the hollow journals were a possible sludge trap, resulting in blocked oil passages and out-of-balance crankshafts. (For these same reasons Rolls-Royce abandoned bored-out shafts in the 1950's.)

In 1936 South Bend adopted all-steel bodies with "turret tops," eliminating body sills, and mounted the bodies directly on the frame. A car's looks were by now as important as its engineering and manufacture. Possibly feeling that Jimmy Hughes' conservatism had rubbed off on the rest of their body design staff, the company showed itself receptive to outside advice, for Raymond Loewy and

1941 President Skyway
Owner: Arno McGraw

Harold S. Vance

1940 Champion
Owner: Ralph E. Dickson

Helen Dryden were retained as consultants from 1936. Helen Dryden's contribution involved interior decor. Of Mr. Loewy, more anon.

By now Studebaker had lost its Caesar of engineering. Barney Roos had got along "rather well" 'with Erskine and "very well" with Paul Hoffman, but he did not hit it off at all with Harold Vance, and since Vance was in the driver's seat and likely to stay there, Barney decided to depart. In 1936 he left for Britain, where he was welcomed with open arms by the Rootes Group, who were busily Americanizing as many components of their cars as possible. This was understandable, since much of Rootes' success came from the distributing of Studebakers. For them Barney devised a variant of his planar front suspension, used on Humber models, and worked on the redesign of the Hillman Minx, Sunbeam Talbot and Humber car program.

For some reason Roos' activities and accomplishments remained a mystery to the British press, and, in fact, years later Laurence Pomeroy actually referred to Barney as "a protégé of Sir William Rootes, who had acted as a consultant to Studebaker and designed their pre-war i.f.s." On returning to the United States Barney joined Willys, and after World War II, having gained much experience from the Jeep, he advised BMC on the constant-velocity joint design for the Mini.

1942 President Skyway Land Cruiser
Owner: Herb Read

Back at South Bend Barney's post was filled by W. S. James, as chief engineer under vice-president of engineering Roy Cole (formerly of Dodge). Their first major task was introducing yet another Studebaker light car. In engineering Studebakers had kept pace with the rest right through the Thirties. But they were still basically thousand-dollar-and-up cars. (How remote even that sounds now!) Despite previous failures as recent as the Erskine and the Rockne, management decided in 1935 to have one more try at the low-priced market (then below $700).

This time they were far more thorough, and they reaped appropriate rewards. The datum line was a study, not of the Big Three cars, but of the people who bought them: more specifically, what these people earned, what they could afford to pay and, most important, how many of them there were, not only at the time of the survey but for several years ahead. It was found that eleven million car owning families had weekly incomes of thirty dollars or less, that their number was increasing at the rate of one million annually and that the automobile accounted for about ten percent of the family budget. "Their ability to operate and maintain their automobiles appeared to be approaching the limit of tolerance," commented Studebaker, noting further that "standard-sized, high quality automobiles which could be operated at low cost were unavailable in the low-priced market primarily because of interchangeability — the practice which allowed a manufacturer to build engines and parts big enough to be used in the production of two or more cars in different price classes." (In this Studebaker was referring to the existing Dictator-Commander-President line, because the arguments which followed showed they had no intention of conceding that the Big Three were either "high quality" or "low cost.")

"Therefore," continued the study, "Studebaker engineers were free to create an entirely new automobile without consideration of interchangeability with other Studebaker models. They started out with a clean sheet of paper to design a car combining high quality, fine performance, and operating costs substantially lower than was afforded by cars in the low price field." This was, incidentally, the last time Studebaker started with a clean sheet. All subsequent "new" Studebakers would use major components — either body or chassis — from previous models.

After some four years development the Champion was unveiled early in 1939. It was apparent that Studebaker engineers had achieved most, if not all, of their objectives. The car weighed 500 to 650 pounds less than any of the Big Three, and Studebaker claimed ten to twenty-five percent more gasoline economy. Considering the low-priced four-door sedan, the rivals compared as follows:

	Champion	Chevrolet	Ford 60	Ford 85	Plymouth
Price:	$740	$689	$665	$705	$726
Wheelbase:	110	112¼	112	112	114
Engine:	L-head 6	OHV 6	L-head V-8	L-head V-8	L-head 6
Bore:	3"	3"	2.6"	3 1/16"	3⅛"
Stroke:	3⅞"	3¾"	3.2"	3¾"	4⅜"
CID:	164.3	216.5	136	221	201.3
BHP:	78	85	60	85	82
RPM:	4000	3200	3500	3800	3200
Axle:	4.55	3.73	4.44	3.78	3.9
Tires:	5.50/16	6.00/16	5.50/16	6.00/16	5.50/16
Weight:	2375	3025	2747	3038	2987
Max. Speed:	75 - 78	75	72	85+	78
Acc.: 10-65 high gear	19.6	19.8	34.8	22.3	24.9
MPG:	20.5	18	19.5	16	—

1950 Commander Starlight
Owner: George W. Mills

The performance figures indicate a miracle. Actually, of course, they were selected by company ad men to show Champion in the best light. In actual fact neither the Champion nor any other car in the group could live for more than a few seconds with a Ford V-8 driver who used his gearbox and took advantage of Henry's mailed fist: the high winding "85" engine and its shattering 65-70 mph second gear performance. But for the careful, economy-minded, "never shift" owner, the Champion *was* something of a miracle, giving him all that a Chevrolet or Plymouth could, with much lower operating costs. It rode as well or better (having the planar i.f.s.), handled easier (there being some 250 pounds *less* on the front wheels), had as much interior room and was at least as well made and reliable.

Although the entire car was new the usual teething period was happy and bug-free. The design had been given the standard pre-production testing over some 300,000 miles at Studebaker's proving grounds and in almost every state of the Union, under all climatic conditions. President Paul Hoffman requested vice-president Cole to carry out further tests after production actually started. The first fifty cars off the line were not shipped to dealers. Instead they were handed over to every engineer and production foreman for a mass test over 10,000 miles during the next two weeks. Daily reports were made to the

1951 Champion
Owner: Thomas A. Ennis

engineering department. After this group test some small defects were corrected and production was resumed. Five more Champions were then taken off the line and driven a total of more than 100,000 miles in six weeks: 20,000 miles per car. On top of this, there was an astonishing 15,000-mile run at Indianapolis in less than 15,000 minutes, and which had been preceded by a twice-across-the-continent trip during which a Champion averaged 40.85 mph and 27.26 mpg over 6144 miles. Admittedly it was overdrive equipped, but still it was a stock car.

"As a result of this action," laconically comments one engineer today, "very few field complaints were received."

This was confirmed at the time by the severest critics. In June of 1940 the Detroit editor of *Iron Age* noted: "The industry has been watching Studebaker's Champion closely. Just the other day an engineer for a competitive corporation revealed privately that his group had completed extensive durability and performance tests on the car and found that it stood up unusually well. At the time, it was being torn down for detailed inspection and the engineers expressed surprise at the quality of various parts and the unusually light weight. Seldom have more favorable comments about a competitor's product been uttered."

Studebaker had spent three and a half million dollars in tooling for the new model. Their confidence paid off, for 72,791 Champions were sold in the first year. Studebaker noted that sales in the initial four months were astonishingly close to the records made by Ford's Model A and the first Plymouth in the late Twenties boom period, despite Studebaker's having only a third to a quarter of the number of retail outlets of these makes. The Champion largely was instrumental in increasing 1939 sales 86.7 percent over 1938, and again in 1940 by 34.3 percent over 1939. Factory employment which had been between 7000 and 8000 increased to 9607 by December, 1939, when Champion manufacture was in full swing. Nineteen forty-one models continued with detail improvements.

In 1942, for the fourth time in their long history, Studebaker went again to war. Their trucks were in demand, they contracted to build aero engines, and they made an original contribution by designing and building the Weasel tracked personnel vehicle — powered by the Champion engine. Their most original contribution of the postwar period was also begun during the war.

Raymond Loewy had been born in Paris in 1893. After studying engineering he emigrated to the United States in 1919. It is interesting to reflect today on one of the first applications of this great industrial designer's talent — decorated dugouts in World War I. He started in America as a fashion designer — ladies underwear — then branched out into advertising, sales promotion and layouts for the big stores. His ability to meticulously supervise every detail from the outer walls of the building to the wrapping of the items sold over the counter earned him the name "the great packager." For the Pennsylvania Railroad he streamlined their gaunt, black locomotives, entering into a lively rivalry with Henry Dreyfus, who was likewise engaged for Pennsy's arch-rival, the New York Central. Before World War II Loewy had won such fame as an industrial designer that the Royal Society of Arts in Britain departed from all precedent and awarded him their "Royal Designer to Industry" diploma. This had never previously been granted to other than British subjects since the founding of the Society in 1754.

It is obvious why Studebaker used Loewy's name in connection with their cars both before the war and after it, but the postwar model which made Loewy super-famous, remade Studebaker's image and ultimately became the orthodox postwar shape was not entirely Loewy's work. The principal designer of one of the most innovative Studebakers built was, to pun his name, an

1951 Commander State
Owner: J. Harold Hendricks

1950 Commander Regal Deluxe   Owner: Harold R. Hendricks

"unknown quantity." But, to follow another pun, "EX" marked the spot where prewar "futuristic, experimental, one-to-five-off" body designs came of age in an actual production automobile — and a mass-produced American one at that. The creator was Virgil M. Exner.

Exner first saw the light of day in Ann Arbor, Michigan, in September, 1909. In his teens he drove Model T's. After four years as chief designer at Pontiac, he joined Studebaker in 1938. The fruits of his association had begun with the 1939-40 models, still worthy of study today for their clean, functional and attractive lines. He had supervised them down to such details as door handles, bumpers and the "S" monogram. His next step, the daring 1947 model, had in one sense been gestating in the minds of automobile engineers for many years.

The advantages of full-width bodies had been appreciated for decades and paper designs had existed even before the First World War. Numerous experimental cars were built in the Twenties and Thirties in both Europe and the United States. As styling exercises, Studebaker themselves had built the forward-looking Pierce Silver Arrows and certain Studebaker models "presaging the future." The European aim was purely technical, as shown in the Jaray and Rumpler designs, where the aerodynamics were studied first and the passengers fitted in afterwards — oftentimes uncomfortably. The American aim was usually passengers first — roomier bodies — as in Stout's Scarabs of 1932-35 (although one of these evidently did have some streamlining merit). Then there were the Tjaarda Sterkenbergs, the Chrysler Airflow and the Czech Tatra — all of which actually got into production (Tjaarda's as the Lincoln Zephyr). These combined advanced styling, aerodynamics and passenger accommodation in one package. But they were not strictly "full width," nor did they bring about a general change in design.

In the 1947 Studebaker, however, all the essentials were combined at the right time so that widespread adoption of the type naturally followed.

Initially, of course, it was highly unorthodox. This writer can still recall his first encounter with one, virtually two years to the day after V-J Day; his first reaction, shared with college classmates who examined it outside a railway station, was that it must have flown in with Buck Rogers at the wheel. It looked like that.

Contemporary with the Studebaker — indeed about six months before it — had been the Frazer and Kaiser, which also had all the elements of today's styles, but lacked the rakishness of Exner's design. In fact, the reaction of one of Harley Earl's team to the Frazer and Kaiser was to prophesy that more designs like that would put the stylist out of business: "No fenders, no stylist."

1952 Commander Starliner
Owner: Lloyd W. Frette

1953 Commander Starline
Owner: Robert M. Poo

954 Commander Starliner
Owner: Bob Ackerwold

1952 Commander Starlight
Owner: William Therber

1954 Conestoga
Owner: Paul Gunder

But Exner retained a vestige of rear fender, outlined it like an inverted checkmark and made it one of his signatures. By inserting touches like this, he showed that the stylist still had plenty of scope.

The "going-both-ways" Studebaker achieved that Model T hallmark of acceptance — people cracked jokes and invented stories about the car. But none of these stories are as interesting as the hitherto unpublished story of how the 1947 Studebaker happened in the first place, told elsewhere in this issue by one of the men who was there to make it happen, Bob Bourke.

Briefly, after his split with Loewy, Virgil Exner carried on his design ideas in the basement of his home. He worked closely with Roy Cole, vice-president of engineering; Eugene Hardig, chief chassis engineer; George Matthews, executive chassis engineer; and Perry Sullivan, chief body engineer. Exner converted his basement to a clay modeling room and one bedroom to a drafting center, and for three months spent weekdays at his regular post at Studebaker and nights and weekends at his improvised design center.

"I employed a full daytime quarter scale clay modeler to carry out design work I had devised the night before," Exner recalled. "The chief body and chassis engineers spent much time working with me. Upon completion of the quarter scale clay it was unanimously approved and shipped (along with me) to

the Budd Company in Philadelphia to be blown up to a full scale wood (painted, trimmed and chromed) mock-up. I supervised all surfacing and finishing of this model at Budd.

"To make a long story short, after this model was shipped to South Bend, a duplicate was built, following exactly the same design — only three inches longer and an inch and a half wider. This became the 'bible' from which all drafts and die models were made. This model was finally 'unwrapped' from secrecy and shown to the Studebaker board and officers, and okayed 100 percent. At this time die models were forty percent complete. . . . As you might guess this whole thing was quite an exciting experience for me and many others of the working group at Stude at South Bend. The toughest problem with the '47 job was the time schedule. This was a 'super' crash program, and could only have been accomplished by a relatively small organization such as Stude.

"I believe the Stude management was strong and more farsighted at the time of decision on the '47 model, and gambled that the 'time was right.' I personally believe that one of the most important factors was that prior to '47 they had Roy Cole as a very capable and active force in all decisions. He was not there in '52, and his successor, Stanwood W. Sparrow, died that year. Also Paul Hoffman had left in 1948."

1954 Commander Starliner
Owner: Marv Silverstein

The car was not styled merely for its looks, striking though they were. The full-width body allowed six inches to be added to the front seat width and ten inches to the rear, and made it a six-passenger car, yet kept overall width below seventy inches. Although not "streamlined" in a wind tunnel sense, the body was aerodynamically superior to any American contemporary and its low drag figure gave economical cruising at highway speeds, particularly if the optional overdrive was specified.

Beneath the speed-lined "Exner" package, of course, the postwar Studebaker was as conventional as other cars. Its chassis engineering at that time needed no revision, although one worthwhile advancement was self-adjusting brakes. These would not be adopted by others for many years.

The car was seven inches lower than the 1946 model and its lower center of gravity improved stability. After trying the 1947 model, Laurence Pomeroy of *The Motor* remarked: "I am bound to say that the stability of the car on bends was markedly in advance of pre-war models. At about 75 mph true speed, one could let the rear wheels drift out in a long slide with the car under perfect control."

The new Champion was as well made as it was well designed, and in postwar export markets, still keen for American cars but glad of economy, the praise equalled that for any previous Studebaker. One South African owner wrote in 1948: "I recently completed a month's trip of 5,000 odd miles with much luggage and five up, two of the passengers being friends from England who frequently remarked en route that the average British car would have dropped to bits if subjected to the battering of corrugations and other bad surfaces, and my only troubles were one broken U-bolt and a filament in a dash light bulb. . . . Petrol consumption is 16 mpg in town and on a long run averaging 45 mph it does over 25 mpg. The water temperature never rises above 170° F., even in great heat on long mountain passes. Springing is comfortable, all seats being within the wheelbase and there is adequate space for six adults. . . . I know that many American cars are unnecessarily showy, but in essentials for this part of the world, quite apart of their general utter reliability, they excel. The body finish is stove baked and withstands the sun and abrasion of dust. Road springs are jacketed to exclude dust and large oil and air filters are standard equipment."

The basic 1947 design was built in three models — the Champion, the Commander and the Land Cruiser, whose wheelbases were 112, 119 and 123 inches. There were two engines, the Champion having its own 3 x 4, 170-cubic-inch unit developing 80 hp at 4000 rpm, the other cars sharing a larger 3 5/16 x 4¾, 246-cubic-inch version of 94 hp. Production of the "new look" models reached 200,000 units in 1949, or 4.1 percent of the market. The percentage was maintained in 1950, though this required an increase to 268,229 cars — the highest figure ever reached by the firm. Their payroll rose to 23,000.

By now the usual three-to-four-year styling revamp was due. This time South Bend chose Loewy to put a new face on the 1950 models. "We gave you the 'New Look'— now we present the 'Next Look'," they said. Actually only the front end and rear fenders were changed, although the change was more than skin deep. The traditional leaf spring i.f.s. was replaced by coils, and automatic transmission introduced in Commanders and Land Cruisers in mid-1950 and in all models for 1951.

Sales in 1951 dropped to 205,000, but the company was still holding four percent of the market, so maybe the Next Look would have better luck Next Year. It was worse. Although a fine modern ohv V-8 was introduced for 1951, sales dropped again to 3.8 percent of the market. As usual the public had begun to tire of a style that was once radical but was now merely facelifted. A similar thing was happening at Hudson.

1956 Sky Hawk
Owner: H. R. Yanz

Studebaker management then considered a new design prepared by Bob Bourke, who was by now chief designer for the Loewy group. This was longer, wider and lower (fifty-four inches high in steel roof form) than the previous models and the overall style was a gorgeous blend of the best features in American and European design. After some arguments, Bourke's coupé and a sedan derivation were accepted, but any idea of a convertible was abandoned. The production coupé was 2 5/16 inches higher than the prototype, but only two inches higher than the contemporary M.G. TD with top up. The sedans, at 60.5 inches, were not low enough for Loewy, but management had insisted on increased headroom. Even so, they were still two inches lower than previous models and remained handsome designs. For style reasons, however, the coupé and hardtop shared the 120½-inch wheelbase with the Land Cruiser, while the Champion and Commander sedans used 116½ inches. Design proportions therefore heavily favored the long wheelbase models, and the public went for them with considerable enthusiasm. Hence the newest problem.

The company had backed themselves into a corner, for they had scheduled high volume production and tooling only for the sedans. The V-8 was used in the medium-priced Commander line and the L-head six continued in the low-priced Champion models. The planned production had been 350,000 annually,

1956 Golden Hawk
Owner: Dr. Gil Zimmerman

with a ratio of three sedans to each coupé. The low production coupé line did not even start until early 1953 — although the cars had been announced in October, 1952 — owing to several bizarre contretemps described anon by Bob Bourke. In the first quarter of 1953, Studebaker's market share fell to 2.4 percent. By December 10th, 1953, the company had built only 183,356 cars instead of the planned 350,000, and sales were running fifty percent sedans and fifty percent coupés — scarcely what had been expected. The first quarter of 1954 saw South Bend's market share drop again to two percent; at mid-year it was down to 1.7 percent.

What was going wrong? One magazine post-mortem titled "Who Killed Studebaker" blamed management and "dead-last engineering." Studebaker's engineering image, they claimed, was "nil." Certainly management had made some mistakes — but they had in the past made many wise decisions as well; Studebaker would not have otherwise survived as long as it did. The charge that the firm completely lacked engineering ability is spurious: They were one of the leading independents and had such features as — to name a few — a modern short-stroke ohv V-8, independent front suspension, automatic overdrive and power steering either before, at the same time as, or just shortly after any of the Big Three. And in a number of cases Studebaker shamed certain imported makes with lofty engineering reputations. Of course, even when it stares it in the face, the Europhile press is oft psychologically incapable of recognizing good sound engineering — if it happens to have "made in the U.S.A." on it. The Hill Holder or automatic overdrive for instance, had they originated in Stuttgart, would have garnered raves instead of yawns.

This writer's theory on the cause of Studebaker's decline at this period is the unfortunate coincidence of cautious management at South Bend and an aggressive man in Dearborn — namely Henry Ford II. So determined was he to recover his grandfather's position as Number One that Henry Ford II stated in the early Fifties he would put Ford in front or break it doing so. So in 1953 the Ford production blitz began. Suddenly Ford stepped up production, shipped the cars to the dealers and told them to sell regardless of price. It was like his grandfather's move some forty years earlier. The dealers had the option of "root, hog or die." They rooted. "No-profit-to-the-dealers" became a permanent way of business. GM naturally reacted vigorously. Cars were discounted by dealers to a mere $100, or even fifty dollars over costs. Big dealerships with huge investments accepted their lot, but the independents had less to lose and less pressure on them, so they simply refused to give their cars away.

Ford failed to achieve either of his objectives — supremacy or bust. Instead he topped Chevrolet occasionally — and busted most of the independents. The latter, however, certainly assisted in the digging of their own graves. In Studebaker's case, the Ford-GM cyclone hit them when they were changing over to a new storm cellar, but they failed to make use of it. The only real chance for survival lay in a shelter big enough for both Studebaker family and its neighbors — Packard, Hudson and Nash.

This had been suggested after World War II — as early as 1946 — by Nash's shrewd, farsighted George Mason. However, after some consideration, Mason at that time had dropped Studebaker from the proposal because it was so deeply rooted in South Bend that removal and centralization would have been difficult, and it already had the highest labor costs in the industry. The latter had plagued Studebaker for years, and contributed substantially to the company's failure.

The possibility of a major amalgam arose again in 1953-54 when Nash and Hudson began serious negotiations that resulted in American Motors. Nance of Packard was interested, but dropped out in favor of a Packard-Studebaker merger. The combination was no good at all for Packard and good only for

1962 Gran Turismo Hawk
Owner: Barbara Langworth

Studebaker as long as Packard's capital lasted. Nance spent Packard money at an unprecedented rate, and since Studebaker consistently lost money during the association, Packard expired in fact in 1956, in fancy in 1958, and in name in 1962. Studebaker followed soon after.

But we are getting ahead of our story. Other changes were taking place at Studebaker. For 1954 the most noticeable styling revision were egg-crate grille inserts, but the company now offered a station wagon bearing a grand old name — Conestoga. In 1955 an urge to mimic certain ungainly rivals resulted in extensive chroming. The Land Cruiser was dropped and the President series added, most spectacular of which was the Speedster, a posh hardtop with leather upholstery, good instrumentation and two- and three-tone paint jobs including the unforgettable "lemon and lime." Mid-year changes included wraparound windshields on sedans and wagons. Options now available included power windows and seats and air conditioning, and Studebaker hired Eleanor La Maire to improve the design of their interiors.

Nineteen fifty-six saw the Speedster give way to the more sporty Hawks, square grilled restyles of the original 1953 coupés. Although excessive in some of their styling, Hawks were always powerful, road gobbling machines of basically good proportions and quality. Leading the 1956 lineup was the Golden

Sherwood H. Egbert

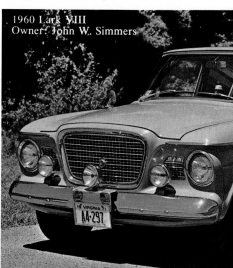

1960 Lark VIII
Owner: John W. Simmers

1961 Lark VIII
Owner: Beg Hamlin

Hawk, a hardtop powered by Packard's 352-cubic-inch V-8, which could approach 120 mph. Next came the hardtop Sky Hawk, with more restrained, unfinned styling and the Studebaker V-8. The Power Hawk (V-8) and Flight Hawk (six), both five-window coupés, rounded out the sporty car lineup, which was significant in that it presaged the four-seat personal car of years to come. But in 1956, sales of 76,545 were down fifty-five percent from 1953. Dealers were lost, those remaining suffered from public reports of their financial condition and enforced merger. Sensing they might be left with orphan cars, the public began to shy off, thereby accelerating sales losses.

Nance resigned in 1956 from the Studebaker-Packard presidency, and Studebaker men, now in control, signed a three-year management contract with Curtiss-Wright, under which the latter gained the use of idle car plants and tax relief on their aircraft profits while Studebaker received further working capital to continue car production. Curtiss sold the Detroit Packard plant and the famous Packard proving grounds at Utica. Studebaker in 1958 even instructed company personnel to sell their Packards and use only Studebakers. Management would have been better employed with more important — and more intelligent — decisions.

For 1957-58 the Hawk line was simplified to the Golden Hawk — now with a supercharged 289 Studebaker V-8 to achieve the same 275 bhp as the Packard engine — and the five-window Silver Hawk coupé. A bare-bones "Scotsman" economy line was introduced, but it didn't help much and was discontinued after 1958. An interesting Starlight hardtop (not a Hawk) was produced in 1958 only, along with the last of the Packard name, comprised of sedan, hardtop, station wagon and Packard Hawk, styled by Duncan McRae with ample help from meddling executives. By 1959, only the pillar-model Hawk remained, though another blow was struck for zestful driving by a four-speed manual gearchange, optional in 1961.

But production continued in a downward spiral, losses mounted. Everybody tried. Curtiss-Wright president Roy Hurley set to curing the over-employment malady, the factory workers themselves had realized the problem. Easy work had been a legend at Studebaker; some Notre Dame students who worked night shifts in the plant claimed they could clear an eight-hour work schedule in two hours. But when employees recognized the seriousness of the company's situation, they rallied round. In 1954 they voted to take a voluntary cut in pay. From then on strikes and bargaining produced an employment pattern competitive with conditions at the Big Three, at least by 1959.

By this time, however, so much ground had been lost that only an inspired

Brooks Stevens prototype Hawk coupé, 1966

1963 Avanti
Owners: Pat and Bruce Slifer

1964 Commander Wagonaire
Owners: Frost & French

1966 Cruiser Daytona
Owner: M. F. Studebaker

— and stable — management could see any hope for a long-term future. One man who did was Harold E. Churchill, who became president in 1956. Churchill had spirit and wisdom that came from a long tenure at South Bend, where he had played a leading role in the development of overdrive. Though a chain smoker, he was a relaxed and patient man, handsome, square-jawed, representing the best tradition of Studebaker automobile men. Churchill had envisioned a substantial role for Packard, which he had hoped to make "the finest car in the highest price field," but by 1957 policy accrued to New York bankers who did not know the automobile business and were hardly sympathetic to Studebaker, let alone Packard. What happened has already been related, and is well known. It was, quite simply, a tragedy.

With Studebaker, Churchill had more success. He aimed at 150,000 cars annually, and by 1959, with the compact Lark, he managed an actual 138,000, creating a 28.5 million dollar profit — the first in five years. Ironically — it must have been bitter knowledge to hard-core Studebaker men — the Studebaker directors were not too pleased. They had other plans for the company — which did not include automobiles. Churchill was an embarrassment. They blocked his plans for new tooling in 1960 and attempted to overrule him by appointing seventy-two-year-old Clarence Francis chairman of the board. Francis was there to take the company out of car production.

The Lark lark was a short-lived triumph. For 1960 the Big Three compacts — Valiant, Falcon and Corvair — invaded the market. Studebaker's profits dropped to less than three-quarter million dollars.

At the board meeting — or uproar — in December of 1960, in a shabby decision reminiscent of earlier ones involving Packard, Churchill was replaced. His successor — on twice the salary — was Sherwood H. Egbert, former vice-president of McCulloch Motors. Egbert, too, felt Studebaker worth fighting for as it was. He took a genuine interest in the cars and moved his home to the Studebaker proving grounds lodge. It was his idea to build the "young image" attention-getting Avanti, certainly one of the more significant milestones of the postwar industry, designed by Loewy's team of Tom Kellog, Bob Andrews and John Ebstein on a forty-day crash program. (See AUTOMOBILE *Quarterly*, Volume I, Number 2 and Volume III, Number 1.)

The Avanti chassis, which had a modified 289 Hawk engine in the 109-inch Lark Daytona convertible chassis was engineered under the supervision of Studebaker's chief, Gene Hardig. Difficulties in getting it into production ruined its chances of large-scale success. Egbert had hoped to sell 20,000 Avantis in 1962, but could only build 1200. However he did enjoy himself driving Avantis up and down the highway between South Bend and the proving grounds at 130 mph — a habit which endeared him neither to the plant staff nor the Indiana State Police.

The Lark meanwhile had become quite a nice package — for all the good that it would do. A convertible and four-door station wagon had been added in 1960; for 1961 the new ohv six-cylinder engine was introduced, developing 112 bhp at 4500 rpm, and the Lark Cruiser appeared at the top of the line. The Lark Daytona was on hand for 1962, with optional four-speed, crisper lines, a well-designed instrument panel and bucket seats, and in 1963 the Avanti "R" series engines were made available for both Larks and Hawks. Disc brakes were optional on all models for 1963, which also saw a really innovative station wagon idea, the Wagonaire, with a sliding roof panel to the rear which permitted the carrying of oversized loads.

The Hawk, too, thankfully, was still with us, as the Gran Turismo Hawk, a clever facelifting by Brooks Stevens on a miniscule budget. Clean limbed, tastefully executed and well trimmed, its basic 1953 coupé body was aborted only by a rather large roof, which Stevens had been forced to use to create real

four-passenger capacity. The G.T. remained until the end of American production. Elegant, well made and fast, it suffered only from an antiquated frame and a demoralized sales force.

Egbert had more extensive plans for Brooks Stevens, who styled three innovative prototypes for family car use for the 1964-66 period, which remain today in Stevens' personal collection. But the end was near.

Production in 1961 had been 78,664 cars, rising to 86,974 in 1962. But over those two years the registration percentage dropped, and the breakeven point was estimated at 120,000 units. For 1963 sales were only 44,000 and $7.5 million was lost in the first six months. Egbert, seriously ill, went on indefinite leave, and in June of 1963 Ralph Guthrie became chairman of the board. In November the production line stopped because it was eighty-six days ahead of sales and 3000 1963 models had still to be cleared from factory inventory. Byers A. Burlingame became president — Studebaker's fifth since 1954. In December of 1963 he announced that the production halt in South Bend was permanent.

In a desperate rear guard action, manufacture was transferred to Studebaker's export plant in Hamilton, Ontario. There it was hoped a yearly production of 20,000 cars — sedans and station wagons only — was viable. It wasn't. At South Bend, engine manufacture continued to employ 1700 of the 6500 production workers, but in August of 1964 that too was finished. At Hamilton operations continued with cars fitted with Chevrolet's 283 V-8 and 230-cubic-inch six, until March of 1966, at which time the doors closed for the Studebaker motorcar, this time forever.

Studebaker-Worthington, as it is now known, is still a large corporation despite the dissolution of its automotive department. While attempting to rehabilitate the car business Egbert had pushed ahead with the diversification which Churchill had begun in 1958. In 1960 seventy-four percent of corporation sales were automobiles, but by 1962 Egbert had changed this to about fifty-fifty. With plants in the United States, Canada and England, Studebaker-Worthington produces aero-space products, gardening and farm equipment, commercial floor polishers, electric generators and refrigerators.

In 1969 this writer was shown around the Studebaker Historical Collection, then in the depressing surroundings of a dingy, unlit brick building in a back street removed from the plant. Tires were flat, many vehicles stood in semi-darkness, and the whole pathetic scene symbolized the tragedy of the Studebaker automobile. Now, however, the exhibits have been relocated to the ground floor of the former Studebaker Administration Building where they can be inspected and photographed by permission of the city engineer. Much credit indeed must be given to the Studebaker Drivers Club, whose members have generously presented or loaned many vehicles to this growing collection. The Michiana Chapter of the club maintains the cars, and tours of the exhibits are always a prime attraction of the organization's annual "Homecoming." It is consoling that despite the final years of heartbreak, some remnant of South Bend's most celebrated product still survives.

One can do a lot of remembering in South Bend. Recalling, for instance, those days when one might disembark from a train at South Bend's Union Station. That once-grand edifice is now deserted, derelict. And Studebaker — now but bare bones. South Bend is not a dying city. But its greatest plant, like Union Station, molders silently in decay. No more does South Bend herald the arrival of *The 20th Century Limited*. No more do the ramps, the production lines, the paint booths, the loading bays, echo to the movement of President Eights, of Skyway sedans, of Starliners, Hawks and Commanders. Both plant and depot are of the past: empty, forlorn, abandoned, forgotten. Remnants of more optimistic days, and of pleasant dreams. ✥

STUDEBA
AS GLADIA
On The Boards, T
& The Sa
by Charles

Those of you familiar with Studebaker only in the modern context may possibly be surprised to discover how thoroughly involved in competition the company once was. In fact, at the time the Studebaker Corporation entered five semi-stock racing cars for the 1932 Indianapolis 500, they had had more experience in the conduct of high-speed record breaking than any other American automobile manufacturer. That's a pretty impressive statement, but one that can be impressively documented as well. During the five years previous Studebaker cars had traveled in excess of 215,000 miles on the fast, steeply-banked board tracks of the nation. Ab Jenkins, the Salt Lake City Mormon who later became famous for his endurance runs on the Bonneville salt flats, had estab-

lished two new transcontinental records for the marque. Glen Shultz, who was affectionately known as "The Old Man of the Mountain" before Louis Unser acquired that title, had won the coveted Penrose Trophy for Studebaker at Pikes Peak. In addition, five Studebaker-powered racing cars had covered more than 2000 miles of actual racing competition in the two previous 500's at Indianapolis. Yes indeed, in competition Studebaker had proved to be a formidable adversary.

But let's take a closer look at the record — from the beginning. It all started in Los Angeles at the Culver City 1¼-mile speedway, where in April of 1927 a Studebaker Commander Six established a plethora of long-distance records:

1526 miles in 24 hours for a 63.60 mph average, 4413 miles in 72 hours for a 61.30 mph average, 5000 miles in 81 hours 48 minutes 22 seconds for a 61.12 mph average. It was a good way to start, but those records were not to remain unchallenged or unbroken for long. During the last week in July two Auburn 8-88's raised the average speed for 5000 miles to 63.695 mph on the new Atlantic City 1½-mile board speedway at Amatol, New Jersey. They also set a new mark of 64.247 mph for the seventy-two-hour period and then established what appeared to be some hard-to-beat records for greater distances: 15,000 miles at a 61.377 mph average and an average of 61.416 for the 240-hour period.

Studebaker would challenge these records, but not right away. First the

Commanders would be tried out on the new Atlantic City speedway on Labor Day, 1927, in a seventy-five-mile stock car race for six-cylinder cars. The two sport roadsters, driven by Ralph Hepburn and Eddie Hearne, walked away from the rest of the field, comprising a brace of Chryslers, a Buick, a Nash, a Hudson and a Star. (The Auburn, being an eight-cylinder car, was not eligible for the event.) Hepburn's Commander crossed the finish line first, averaging nearly 86 mph, almost a minute ahead of Hearne's sister car. Later in the month the same pair were joined by a third Commander, to be driven by Ab Jenkins, at Charlotte, North Carolina. The program on that 1¼-mile board speedway included a seventy-five-mile event limited to six-cylinder stock cars costing $2000 or less, to be run concurrently with a 125-mile free-for-all stock car race. Ralph Hepburn repeated his previous victory at Atlantic City, this time increasing his average to better than 88.5 mph, Eddie Hearne finished second and Ab Jenkins' Commander finished last. Lest this seem a discredit to Jenkins' performance, it should be mentioned that Studebakers were the only entrants in the event. Originally the seventy-five miler was to have included competition from Buick, Hudson, Chrysler and Nash, but after the three Commanders had qualified at better than 85 mph, all the other entrants summarily withdrew from the contest. The Studebakers finished the race in perfect condition without a pit stop and were pronounced stock by the Technical Committee of the AAA Contest Board, which at the time permitted removal of fenders, windshield, top, lights, spare wheel and muffler.

These two victories convinced Studebaker that some record breaking was now in order, and the Commanders were returned to the Atlantic City speedway for a twenty-four-hour run against the clock. Three well-known racing drivers — Ralph Hepburn, Harry Hartz and Jimmy Gleason — were selected to handle the single car that was to go after the record. The run was made October 6th and 7th, with the car carrying standard equipment, including windshield, fenders, lights, top, spare wheel and muffler. Thusly outfitted, the Commander succeeded in breaking the former record for stock cars in its class by more than 100 miles, averaging 75.623 mph for the twenty-four-hour period.

Following that successful run, two Dictators, a coupé and a sedan, were readied for twenty-four-hour runs to be staged October 10th and 11th. These were smaller, less expensive cars selling for under $1400. Some Studebaker test drivers augmented the three veteran racers who had established the Commander record, and this crew established average speeds better than 60 mph for both Dictators, the sedan covering 1483 miles. At the same time an Erskine sedan was sent out to seek a twenty-four-hour speed record for cars selling at less than $1000. At the end of its stint the Erskine had reeled off close to 1300 miles, an extraordinary performance for a small car which had trouble seeing 60 mph on the speedometer.

A week later at Atlantic City three Commanders stood poised on the starting line, daring to break the Auburn 15,000-mile record. They not only accomplished that, but then went on to establish new records up to 25,000 miles. The two sport roadsters averaged better than 65 mph, and the sedan, which had flipped on the icy boards during one of the night runs and had been hurriedly repaired, averaged almost 62 mph. Upon the conclusion of this long test of endurance at high speed, the cars were checked — part by part — against other Studebakers taken directly from dealers' showrooms, as well as against published specifications, to assure that they were strictly stock automobiles, similiar in every respect to those available at any showroom. They were.

Due to the weather all further tests at the Atlantic City speedway were postponed until the end of April the following year. Then two Dictator roadsters were each sent away on a 5000-mile run. The faster of the two completed the distance in 79 hours 11 minutes, an average speed of 63.138 mph, raising its former twenty-four-hour mark by better than one mile per hour. The second Dictator averaged better than 61 mph. For models selling under $1400, these were formidable long distance records for stock cars.

Further record breaking followed that summer, as four Studebaker Presidents put up a 30,000-mile run at Atlantic City. The eight-cylinder cars — two roadsters and two sedans — had been chosen at random from factory production lines, fully equipped including spare wheel and tire. For nineteen days and nights, in mid-July when the temperature soared to a high of 90 degrees and often fell as low as 50 degrees at night, the Presidents went whirling on and on, pitting only briefly every four hours for fuel and oil, a tire check, a look at the water and a fresh driver. Studebaker personnel and AAA officials were amazed at the consistent performance of the two roadsters which were so evenly matched that only three minutes separated them at the finish. Their elapsed times were 26,326 and 26,329 minutes, a truly remarkable average speed of 68.37 mph. Even the sedans averaged more than 60 mph for 30,000 miles!

Later in the year two President sport roadsters were dispatched to capture the twenty-four-hour record. One of the cars would be teamed by Russell Snowberger, Zeke Meyer, Ralph Hepburn and Bob McDonough, these noted racing drivers to pilot the car each in turn. Ab Jenkins, at the wheel of the second Studebaker, had elected to drive the full distance without an alternate, his first twenty-four-hour solo run in a stock car. This cadre of cars and drivers proceeded to establish twelve new stock car marks for one, three, six, twelve and twenty-four hours, and for five, ten, fifty, 100, 500, 1000 and 2000 miles. The first car covered 2044.8 miles in twenty-four hours for an average speed of 85.2 mph, while Jenkins' solo mark was only slightly slower. These new records, in addition to the 102 long distance marks established earlier in the year, gave Studebaker a total of 114 stock car records in 1928, thirty-one of which would still be unbroken some three and a half decades later.

Meanwhile Pikes Peak continued to beckon. Studebaker had first journeyed to the mountain in 1923 with the entry of a Studebaker Special roadster to be driven by Charles H. "Chuck" Myers, a Colorado Springs native in his first competition appearance at Pikes Peak. Myers scored a first place win that year in Event No. 3 (for engines over 300 cubic inches and cars weighing up to 2000 pounds), and returned the following year to repeat the triumph with a fastest time of 18 minutes 15.4 seconds. (The Studebaker Special of 1923 is sometimes referred to as the Van Dyke Special for 1924, but they were one and the same car.) By 1927 Myers was facing stiff competition from the powerful eight-cylinder likes of Stutz and Auburn, but he nevertheless made a spectacular climb to capture second fastest time of the day, only forty-eight seconds behind the Stutz and fifty-one seconds ahead of the Auburn.

It was in 1927, too, that the AAA Contest Board became interested in the mountain; the Penrose Trophy for the fastest time up Pikes Peak would for seven years henceforward be awarded to the swiftest stock car. By regulation entries had to be chosen at random from factory production models, initially with the option of removing lamps, fenders, running boards, top, windshield, spare tire and muffler, though by 1929 the Contest Board had changed their mind about that and decreed all stock cars must carry full standard equipment. Studebaker was happy to comply, plucking two Presidents and one Commander — eight-cylinder models all — from the production line, thereafter duly impounded by the Contest Board. Glen Shultz, at that time the most consistent winner at the Peak, was assigned to drive one of the Presidents, Ab Jenkins the other. Ralph Hepburn was to drive the Commander. The trio performed spectacularly. Shultz lived up to all expectations, setting a new record of 21 minutes 43.40 seconds, a time almost two seconds better than the former Auburn

Two Dictators come into a banked curve during a 5000-mile nonstop run at the Atlantic City Speedway in April, 1928. Below: The fastest Dictator is flagged at the finish line.

record. Jenkins' President finished second, Hepburn's Commander third. A clean sweep for Studebaker.

The 12.6-mile climb to the Peak in 1931 saw Chuck Myers return to the "Special" racing division with a car called the Hunt Special. Powered by a modified President Eight engine, it had been designed and built jointly by George Hunt, supervisor of Studebaker test facilities, and Ab Jenkins for the Indianapolis 500. Piloted by Tony Gulotta in that event, the car was on lap 158, running second to leader Billy Arnold, when the latter lost a wheel and hit the wall. Gulotta was in the lead for two laps, until Lou Schneider, the eventual winner, passed him — and in his effort to catch the new leader Gulotta lost control and also went to the wall, ironically in the same spot where Arnold had spun. Afterwards the Hunt Special was rebuilt and shipped to Colorado Springs where Chuck Myers had considerably better luck, making fastest time of the day up Pikes Peak and establishing a new record of 17 minutes 10.3 seconds in the "Special" division.

The revisions made for 1930 to the regulations governing the Indianapolis 500 (making the two-man racing body mandatory and permitting the use of stock car engine blocks up to 366 cubic inches) brought the Studebaker presence to the Hoosier capital. For the '30 event, Russell Snowberger devised a racing car utilizing a modified Studebaker President Eight engine, fitted with

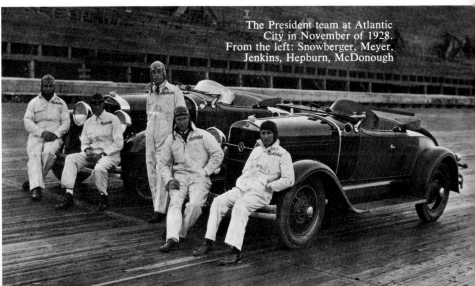

The President team at Atlantic City in November of 1928. From the left: Snowberger, Meyer, Jenkins, Hepburn, McDonough

Chuck Myers and the Hunt Special: Pikes Peak, 1931

four Winfield downdraft carburetors and a Bosch magneto. Dubbed the Russell Eight Special, the car was driven by Snowberger to an eighth place finish at a 89.166 mph average. Reportedly the car cost a mere $1500, and this included the Studebaker engine. If this strains incredulity, consider also that another report contends Snowberger completed the championship circuit that year in third place — and with a total repair bill of less than two dollars! Incidentally, Snowberger entered the same car in the 1931 500 and finished fifth with an average speed of 94.090 mph.

The 1930 Indianapolis rule changes had also stirred competition fever among a number of Studebaker engineering department employees. Accordingly a group of these men — William Richards, George Onishi, J. C. MacDonald, Joseph Tate and Ernie Huntley — teamed to work up a car for the 500 that year. According to E. T. Reynolds, former assistant to the vice-president and chief engineer at Studebaker: "The car was basically a shortened Studebaker President Eight chassis using a modified President straight-eight 336-cubic-inch engine. It was christened the Romthe Special — the name being coined from the first letter of the last name of each of the sponsors, with the 'e' being added merely to make it phonetic. Driver of the Romthe was to be Luther Johnson, in whose garage the car was being built. Johnson, a Studebaker test driver and experimental mechanic, had been doing considerable racing of Studebaker stock

cars and winning consistently. However, when Ernie Huntley allowed his girlfriend to sit in the seat of the car, Johnson, true to the superstitions of the racing fraternity, refused to drive it in the race. MacDonald, one of the sponsors and also a Studebaker test driver, then took over as driver and qualified the car for the race. It ran well until being forced to withdraw on the 112th lap due to a split seam in the fuel tank."

The Romthe Special was rechristened the Richards Special for the 1931 500, this time with Luther Johnson at the wheel. Once more, ill luck. When Billy Arnold spun in the northwest turn, Johnson could not avoid him, smacking him broadside. E. T. Reynolds recalls: "Arnold took out thirty feet of concrete wall while the Richards Special rode the top of the wall backwards for nearly 300 feet, falling on the off-track side just short of Grandstand H, from where Johnson's wife was watching in paralyzed terror. Neither Johnson nor his mechanic was seriously injured."

Studebaker Corporation decided to get into the act themselves in 1932, building five Studebaker Specials for the 500 that year. The 1931 Hunt Special served as the prototype and in fact became one of the team cars. Frames and bodies for the racers were built in Indianapolis by Herman Rigling, a German artisan in metal. Brakes, axles and other chassis components were plucked from stock, and the Studebaker assembly line provided the engine parts, the powerplants then being put together in the engineering garage. Magnetos were substituted for the standard distributors, fans and generators were eliminated and replacing the single updraft carburetors were four downdraft variations with special manifolding and balancing tubes. Otherwise the engines were strictly standard, the resulting racers fitting in the so-called "85% stock" category.

In the 500 the Studebaker Special driven by Cliff Bergere finished in third spot at an average speed of 102.66 mph, the first time a semi-stock car had ever completed the event at better than 100 mph — and the car was only 1.482 mph slower than Fred Frame's winning Miller-Hartz Special, an out-and-out racing car. Second place went to Howdy Wilcox in a Miller. Cliff Bergere recalls that after the event, upon entering the Miller garage, "someone brushed against the Pitman arm — and it fell off!" Had that happened to the Miller during the race, it would have put good old No. 22 in second instead of third!

Coming from a thirty-eighth starting position (yes, there were forty starters in 1932, forty-two in 1933), Zeke Meyer drove his Studebaker Special to sixth place, averaging 98.476 mph, while Tony Gulotta finished thirteenth with his, being flagged on the completion of 184 laps.

According to E. T. Reynolds, the cars might have performed even better, save for one unfortunate decision: "Just before the race the team manager became apprehensive that tire wear might be greater than previously anticipated and accordingly he borrowed some extra wheels and tires from another stable. What he was not aware of was that the taper on the outer ends of the hubs of the borrowed wheels was such that when the Studebaker knock-off caps were tightened, the point of contact was on the spokes of the wheel, instead of against the hub. As a result, the Studebaker Specials began losing wheels shortly after leaving the pits following each tire change as the knock-off caps would work loose. Considerable time was lost by all five cars before the difficulty was diagnosed and corrected."

Peter Kreis' Studebaker Special was wrecked on lap 178 and awarded fifteenth place, while Luther Johnson's car lost a wheel on lap 165 and was awarded sixteenth spot. Of the other Studebaker-powered cars riding in the 1932 500, Malcolm Fox broke a spring in the Richards Special on lap 135 and was awarded twentieth place, "Doc" MacKenzie in the Brady Special was out on lap 66 with engine trouble, while Al Aspen in the Brady and Nardy Special

The Studebaker team at Indianapolis, 1932

suffered a broken connecting rod on lap 31.

For 1933 the Studebaker Corporation decided on a body redesign with a view to reducing wind resistance and gaining a few precious miles per hour speed. Again quoting E. T. Reynolds: "Wood models of the proposed design were sent to the University of Michigan for testing in their wind tunnel. This probably was the first such scientific approach to the problem of wind resistance made on cars designed for the Indianapolis track. Earlier, any such studies had been confined principally to cars intended for assaults on the world land speed record for the measured mile. Body design was finally approved, and Herman Rigling was commissioned to build new bodies for four of the cars; the fifth car, No. 37, still belonging to Ab Jenkins, was not included. The engine of Jenkins' car, however, was moved ahead eight inches to coincide with the other four. Tail section of the body was lengthened to compensate for having moved the rest of the body forward in line with the engine. One of the new radiator shells and grilles was used.

"Considerable research work on the engines was done during this period with a view to increasing their output. No records remain of the details of these studies. However, the 1933 cars were equipped with higher compression cylinder heads and different camshafts than the 1932 versions. Also a change was made in carburetion from Winfield to Stromberg. The use of Scintilla magnetos was continued, but an improved model was used. The nineteen-inch wheels used in 1932 were cut down to eighteen inches, using the original hubs, and 7.00-inch tires were substituted for the 6.50's used the year before. Steel discs, designed to cover the wire wheels, were quickly eliminated when the cars became unwieldy in cross-winds."

The Studebaker Specials performed well during practice prior to qualification for the 1933 500. The fastest car was that driven by Cliff Bergere who put up an average of 115.643 for his ten-lap qualifying run for the pole position in the fourth row of the starting lineup. Slowest qualifier of the Studebaker team was Luther Johnson at a 110.097 mph average, putting him in the outside position in the seventh row. Finally race day came. A drivers' strike over the eligibility of one of their number caused an hour's delay, and by the time the field was on its way a torrid Indiana sun was blazing down on the bricks.

Unfortunately the beautifully streamlined Studebakers soon developed a fault that neither the designers had foreseen nor the wind tunnel tests disclosed. As E. T. Reynolds explained, the air flowed over and around the bulbous bodies in breathtaking fashion, but none got into the cockpit: "As the sun rose higher in the sky and the tempo of the race increased, the heat and lack of air circulation in the cockpits became unbearable for the drivers and their riding mechanics. One after another, the four streamlined cars came into the pits . . . and slits [were quickly cut] in the sides of the bodies to provide ventilation."

All five Studebaker Specials completed the full 200 laps, three of them in the money. Tony Gulotta made the best showing, finishing in seventh place, averaging 99.071 mph. Zeke Meyer came in ninth, Luther Johnson tenth, Cliff Bergere eleventh and L. L. Corum twelfth. Two other Studebaker-powered cars finished among the first ten, the Art Rose Special driven by Dave Evans finished in sixth place, while Russ Snowberger placed his trusty Russell Eight Special in eighth spot.

The only other appearance of the 1933 Indianapolis-type Studebaker Specials was at the revival of the famous road race held at Elgin, Illinois, in August. Run as an attraction for visitors to the Century of Progress Exposition at Chicago, this revival consisted of two events: first, a stock car event, and second, a special racing car contest. Each race consisted of twenty-five laps around the old, original 8.1-mile road course, the full distance being 202.5 miles.

Cliff Bergere placing third in the 1932 500

Studebaker did not enter any cars for the stock event, but two of the Indianapolis racers participated in the second contest. Dave Evans piloted the Studebaker driven by Tony Gulotta in the 500 and during the race was timed at 135 mph as he sped past the judges stand. He finished sixth, while the other Studebaker Special, driven by Lou Moore, came in seventh. Another Studebaker-powered car, the famous Russell Eight Special, this time driven by Mauri Rose, placed third with an average of 85.60 mph.

The Studebaker Corporation withdrew from racing after the Elgin event of 1933, but Studebaker-powered "specials" continued to make a good showing in the Indianapolis 500 for the next four years. In the 1934 running, Russell Snowberger once again drove the Russell Eight Special to eighth place, averaging 97.297 mph. In 1935 both Harris Insinger's Cresco Special and Jimmy Snyder's Blue Prelude Special were powered by 336-cubic-inch Studebaker eight-cylinder engines, Insinger's car being awarded fourteenth place after being flagged on lap 185, while Snyder's mount suffered a broken spring and was sidelined on lap 97. Frank Brisko, driving the Art Rose Special, a front wheel drive chassis with a 250-cubic-inch Studebaker eight-cylinder engine, was forced out on lap 57 with a broken universal joint. In 1936 Zeke Meyer was behind the wheel of the Boyle Products Special (which may have been the Art Rose Special of the year previous) which he piloted to ninth place at 101.331 mph.

Pit stop at Indy, 1933

Ab Jenkins and the Sheriff

Ab Jenkins, Paul Hoffman and the cross-country Commander

The following year Louis Tomei drove the Sobonite Special (which was the car driven in the 500 in 1932 by Cliff Bergere), finishing tenth with an average speed of 101.825 mph.

As enticing as were the boards, the bricks and the mountain during this decade of Studebaker competition, no less alluring was the challenge of the transcontinental. Indeed a cross-country record was among the first garnered by Studebaker Corporation. This was in June of 1926 when Ab Jenkins and a Studebaker "Sheriff" took on L. B. Miller's mark with a Wills Sainte Claire, lowering the record some sixteen hours with a 3471-mile jaunt from New York to San Francisco completed in 86 hours 20 minutes. Two months later it was Miller's turn, as he settled himself behind the wheel of a Wills Sainte Claire and proceeded to clip 3 hours·8 minutes off the Studebaker record in a 3368-mile trek from San Francisco to New York. The following year — in September — Ab Jenkins and a Commander Six sedan started in New York and 77 hours 40 minutes later pulled into San Francisco to bring the record back to Studebaker. The rivalry ended there. Thereafter Miller switched to a Chrysler for a twice-across-the-continent record but Studebaker didn't bother to recipro-cate. Some twelve years later, however, a Studebaker Champion was driven 3076 miles coast to coast in about seventy-five hours and what was primarily an economy run. The car then trekked back across the continent. The results were praiseworthy indeed; averaging 600 miles per day, the fuel consumption for the Champion was a almost unbelievable 27.26 miles per gallon. This same car was then taken to the Indianapolis Speedway where it was driven continu-ously for 15,000 miles, averaging 62.02 mph and 19.34 mpg.

The early Sixties found Studebaker automobiles in yet another record break-ing venture, as related by the dynamic Andy Granatelli in his book, *They Call Me Mister 500.* Suffice it to say here that initially, in August of 1962, he set a flying mile record of 168.15 mph and a standing mile record of 92.03 mph in a supercharged Avanti at the Bonneville salt flats, those marks being the average speed of runs made in two directions. The following summer further records fell as two young women, Paula Murphy and Barbara Nieland drove an Avanti equipped with Sears Allstate tires from Los Angeles to New York in 49 hours 36 minutes and New York to San Diego in 52 hours 6 minutes.

October that year at Bonneville found Andy Granatelli, his brothers Joe and Vince, the ladies Murphy and Nieland, a team of twenty mechanics and, as An-dy put it, "new Studebakers scattered all the way to the horizon." The cars — 1964 models numbering twelve in all — ranged from the company's thriftiest little six-cylinder version to an experimental Avanti called Due Cento, and in-cluded convertibles, hardtops, a pair of strictly stock Avantis and some run-of-the-mill two-doors. Engines, in addition to the small six and the double-

Avantis scorched the salt at Bonneville in October of 1963, with the help of the Granatelli corps and others. Here Bill Burke has his turn, driving to a 147.36 mph record in the E-Supercharged class.

The cross-country Avanti

supercharged experimental 304.5-cubic-inch V-8 of the Due Cento, included the standard single-supercharged V-8 of 289 cubic inches, the high performance 304.5-cubic-inch single-supercharged R-3 and a new powerplant, the R-4, a 304.5-cubic-inch unblown V-8 with two big four-barrel carburetors mounted on a special manifold.

In an endurance run of ten hours duration, the two young women alternated behind the wheel of a Studebaker Commander Six from dawn to dusk to grind off 1000 miles at an average speed of 100.29 mph. The run was made on a very soft and greasy ten-mile circle course recently mushed up by a rainstorm and wrested the long-standing record held by John Cobb who had driven a Hudson Six for Class D records back in 1939. The day following Barbara teamed with Vince Granatelli in a Studebaker Daytona convertible fitted with an R-4 engine, setting a new record of 118.33 mph for 500 kilometers, breaking the marks set by Bill Taylor in a 1954 Dodge and by Danny Eames in a 1957 Ford.

On Wednesday, October 22nd, the Granatelli brothers Joe and Vince piloted a supercharged convertible to a speed of 146 mph for 100 miles and 140.45 mph for 500 miles. Then as night began to fall, the brothers wheeled out Paula's old reliable Avanti for a practice session. Andy failed to get enough traction for a decent lap time; then Vince tried and spun out badly in a soft

spot. Finally Joe, the eldest brother, took the car and held it in the groove so well he kept right on running and ended by breaking ten records previously held by a Pontiac Catalina which had been driven by Mickey Thompson. These ranged from twenty-five through seventy-five kilometers, with flying and standing starts, and included a flying fifty-kilometer average of 155 mph flat. In an appropriate finale, Andy Granatelli drove an R-3 Avanti to break the former year-old Studebaker records for the American Class C Closed Car Supercharged and American Unlimited Class Closed Car categories, clocking averages up to 170.8 mph for all distances from one kilometer through ten miles.

What remains today from this flurry of Studebaker competitive activity through the years is largely nostalgia — and some of the historic Studebaker racing cars themselves. The five Studebaker Specials of the early Thirties have been of most interest to historians. What happened to them? They were raced, as we've seen, after the 1933 500 — and at least one of them turned up at the Studebaker exhibit at the Century of Progress in Chicago that year. Later two of the cars were sold to a syndicate and shipped to South America, one being lost at sea en route, the other destroyed by fire following an accident at an Argentine track. The Ab Jenkins Special, No. 47, was transported to Utah where it was used a while as a sports car by Jenkins' son, and was later purchased by Ray R. Donald of Balboa, California, who according to most recent reports is considering offering it for sale. Special No. 34 — the Tony Gulotta car — turned up in a salvage yard in Wisconsin in 1961, discovered there by Brooks Stevens. He purchased the car, restored it to its 1933 configuration and today it is on display at his fine automobile museum just north of Milwaukee.

The history of the remaining Studebaker Special — Cliff Bergere's No. 22 — is the most complete. It changed hands a number of times — a South Bend lumber dealer by the name of Dan Sanders had it a while, then Virgil Exner who converted it into a sports car for road use, then Brett Wood of Piqua, Ohio — before returning to Studebaker Corporation. The repurchase by Studebaker was for the company's centennial celebration in 1952, and the car appeared during the pre-race activities at Indianapolis, a Studebaker Commander serving as pace car that year. Subsequently it was stored in one of the old wagon-making buildings at South Bend.

A decade later when a Studebaker again paced the field for the Indianapolis 500, No. 22 was back. It had earlier been suggested that the car be restored for the pre-race activities attendant to the 1962 running of the Indy classic — and Studebaker president Sherwood H. Egbert readily concurred, providing the restoration be authentic and the car capable of coming down Indy's main stretch at no less than 120 mph. Luther Johnson, whose service as a Studebaker experimental mechanic now approached the thirty-five-year mark, saw to it. After restoration, Studebaker Special No. 22 was taken to Studebaker's proving grounds where it hit speeds in the neighborhood of 140. On completion of several exhibition runs at Indianapolis in 1962, it was once again put in storage on the fourth floor of one of the old Studebaker factory buildings, together with a variety of historic Studebaker vehicles dating back to the company's Nineteenth Century years.

Today the City of South Bend houses an impressive collection of Studebakers, including the Conestoga wagon which carried the Studebaker family west from Pennsylvania in 1835, the landau built for President Grant in 1873, a Studebaker Electric of 1902, the "transcontinental" Commander of 1927, the 1964 Daytona which was the last Studebaker manufactured in the South Bend plant, and many, many others: an altogether splendid assemblage. But Studebaker Special No. 22 is not there. Instead it is owned today by Andy Granatelli's STP Corporation. Somehow that seems quite appropriate too.✿

The elegant Studebaker Starliners of 1953 and 1954 were without doubt milestones of the very highest order: Simple, refined, beautiful from every angle, they remain today flawless designs that are increasingly sought after by those wise enough to invest in a sleeper when they see one. For the Starliner is not — yet — an expensive proposition. Among Studebaker enthusiasts it has been upstaged for years by the Avanti and Hawks, though in all honesty its utterly pure lines surpass both in many ways.

Bob Bourke, in an indirect sort of way, designed the Starliners. He was with Studebaker from just before the Second World War up through 1955, participating in and heading up many of those wonderful styling projects created by South Bend. He is, as you will learn, a rather self-deprecating individual — a rare trait among men of any calling — and several may take issue with his evaluation of, for instance, his Starliner-based sedans, which look a whole lot better than Bob says they do when compared with the bloated, graceless blobs with which they shared our domestic market.

Starlight, Starliner, Hawk: here is their story, the way they happened, told by one who saw it all.

I think if you talk to any of the designers who were with me at South Bend after the Second World War you'll find that, like me, the things they remember most are the good times. Despite occasional disagreements there was a lot of camaraderie, and while some of the things we designed are better left to memory, we enjoyed our work with Studebaker immensely. For each of us, I feel, the idea that the Starliner and its derivations would someday become as sought after as AUTOMOBILE *Quarterly* tells me they are was the last thing in our minds. Now that we're all a lot older and wiser we look back on our South Bend days with a mixture of nostalgia and regret: nostalgia for the times we had, regret that some designs and ideas were not put into production and that others — better forgotten — were.

As far as industrial design goes, my own story began in Chicago with Sears, Roebuck in the mid-Thirties. I worked there for four years, designing such memorable devices as manure spreaders, power tools, outboard motors, radio cabinets, washing machines and Coldspot refrigerators — the nearest I came to cars were the manure spreaders: At least they had wheels. I had always wanted to design automobiles though, and an opportunity to show Virgil Exner my portfolio culminated in my being hired by Studebaker prior to Pearl Harbor. Virg was assigned to South Bend under Loewy, who was already firmly established as Studebaker's chief design consultant, having been credited with the very fine Champion of 1939.

It wasn't long before the war came, and men with drafting or engineering experience were needed for the defense effort. A special division for new aircraft engine development was established at Studebaker by Curtiss-Wright, and I was soon hired by the latter to participate in design and testing of the new air-cooled turbocharged engine for the Army Air Corps. In initial stages the engine developed 300 horsepower from a single cylinder which, by the way, had an eight and a half inch bore. Test engine multiples of two cylinders were next, with the final goal being 8000 horsepower. The engine was to have been mounted in an airplane fuselage for service, driving four props on the wings. However, toward the end of the war jet engine design breakthroughs brought a halt to the program and I began, happily, designing cars again.

During this period I worked once more with Virgil Exner. "Ex" and I, and an excellent modeler named Frank Alhroth, began the initial work on the 1947 program which was to end with an all-new postwar car. (The design characteristics of the 1947 model would incorporate the first flush front fender and wraparound rear window.) Virg's boss, Raymond Loewy, was meanwhile evaluating what I could do, and finally asked if I'd like to join his team. Loewy was under contract to provide designs for Studebaker; Exner and Alhroth were the only other personnel from Loewy's assigned to South Bend, while I was working directly for Studebaker. I was delighted to accept "R.L.'s" offer. I'd always admired him, especially for his ability to sell advanced designs to recalcitrant executives. It was all really only a formality though, as I continued working with Ex and Frank on the 1947 proposals. Loewy, meanwhile, was busy convincing management to accept these designs for the postwar era.

Before the Starlight was finished, Exner's employment by Loewy terminated, basically over a disagreement in philosophy and approach. Ex felt that a man was either a designer or a promoter, but not both, and to make matters worse he felt Loewy received all the credit from both management and the public. Although I understood Ex's viewpoint, I still held R.L. in high regard as I recognized the necessity of being a good salesman in this profession. Mr. Loewy also had, and still has, a great "eye." While he may not have created a certain design, line or contour, he knew instinctively when a designer had better than average talent and drive, and he would always bring out the best that designer had to offer for the client. As I know him, R.L. is a diligent, intelligent and fair man, proven by his many successes in his field.

Immediately after Ex and Loewy agreed to disagree, Roy Cole, Studebaker's vice-president in charge of engineering and an enthusiastic Exner backer, set Virg up as a sort of rival designer to the Loewy group. Ex took most of the materials we had developed prior to the split and went to work again at home in his basement, competing directly with the Loewy offerings. Gordon Buehrig relieved Ex as chief of the Loewy design team and both sides began competing for the final 1947 line of production cars.

Not surprisingly, most of our ideas were pretty much in line with each other's. Ex was working along principles he and I had previously developed with Loewy, and we were moving along similar lines. But Roy Cole was a decided influence, and he presented Exner's renderings to management personally. Studebaker bought them, and Ex thereby did the final design work for the 1947 Champion and Commander lines, which included the famous Starlight coupé, one of the first truly postwar automobile designs.

About a year later Gordon Buehrig left and Mr. Loewy asked me to take his place. My title became manager and chief designer, and my group at maximum was comprised of forty people including designers, modelers, woodworkers and pattern makers. Of that total, about ten were designers.

Loewy was determined to win back the Studebaker production contract, and the first new thing we developed was the famous spinner-nosed Studebaker for 1950. A lot of people thought this design was copied from the Tucker, but in reality it evolved quite separately. Roy Cole, of course, was feeding Exner engineering information — what could be done to the chassis and such — just a little bit in advance of us, and Loewy suddenly got wind of a redesign Ex was creating for the 1950 line. R.L. came to me and said we'd have to have a competitive presentation ready within four weeks.

I remember Mr. Loewy to this day, with his French accent, saying, "Now Bob, eet has to look like ze aeroplane." He wanted a spinner motif to be the principal appearance feature of the front end. This idea was under development prior to the introduction of the spinner-grilled '49 Ford which I also had a hand in, but that's another story. At this time, Lord help me, I said, "Yes sir, Mr. Loewy! We'll put that spinner smack out in front" — and we did.

Originally we were allowed to change the cowl, which contributed significantly to the general front end configuration. But in the end we were forced, to our dismay, to work with the cowl and windshield from earlier models. We did manage to get our hood down relatively low, and the spinner itself was not overly gaudy in its original concept, having a machined and light detail appearance. Originally the fenders were capped with chrome at the bottom and the bumper conformed to the whole frontal shape, but they couldn't build such bumpers economically. We reverted to straight versions with four-inch-diameter tubes covering the bumper support bars. I shudder when I look at a '50 or a '51 now, but in those days, for what they were, I guess they weren't too bad. Besides, the Loewy team won the styling contest this time, putting us even with Ex again, so it was cause for rejoicing. R.L. celebrated the occasion by putting a propeller on the nose of his personal car which revolved majestically in the breeze — like ze aeroplane.

The 1953 "Loewy coupé"— or rather what was to be called the Loewy coupé — began in the early spring of 1951, but was originally scheduled as a show car: a one-off, handmade, no-tooling special for the forthcoming round of automobile shows. At the start I spent considerable time with Gene Hardig, chief chassis engineer, developing revised seating and interior dimensions from existing production chassis and lowering the roof to give the automobile a chance to end up with relatively good proportions. Four of my designers were given a free hand in creating their concept of a new body form, sketching and then building quarter-scale clay models. At the same time I worked on my own quarter-scale model, developing two different concepts, one on each side. At a review of the models we decided to develop this last as a full-size clay model which would again be split into two concepts, the driver's and passenger's sides being different. Mr. Loewy at this time left the States to visit to his various design offices in other countries, and I was given a completely free hand to proceed with the car's development. The work load at this time was fantastic; we had design development programs covering standard bread-and-butter type production sedans as well as truck programs — all with deadlines looming. My burning desire to design a car with a completely free hand, with so little time, required a fourteen-hour day seven days a week, and on many occasions two- and three-day stands of uninterrupted work without sleep. But I was encouraged by visits after hours by Paul G. Hoffman and Harold Vance, the two gentlemen who had, as a team, put Studebaker back on its feet after Mr. Erskine's reign.

Loewy team: at first table, Bourke (L) and Exner; Koto behind, Buehrig at chart.

Under my supervision both sides of the coupé began to take form. Holden "Bob" Koto, working as my assistant with help from Hugh Bush, Don Hein and Fred Horning, worked out the right side of the full-size clay. Aided by John Lutz and John Bird, my chief modeler and overall supervisor of modeling respectively, I tackled surface development and details on the left side. Bob Koto worked diligently on his side and incorporated a number of good contour and design criteria from our preliminary quarter-scale models. As for me, this was a rare opportunity to show what I could do. In the back of my mind all along was the thought that if the result was practical enough, and well designed, it might have some production potential. I designed it with that in mind — the wraparound rear window, for example, was curved in a manner that I had previously insured was possible for glass manufacturers to duplicate in quantity.

On my original model there was no rear quarter window. The door glass from the vent wing back was one piece, and designed to crank fully down. The door itself was large for those days. The lack of a rear quarter window gave the car a much cleaner appearance, the same principle being used on present-day Camaro and Firebird bodies. It didn't end up that way in the Starliner's case, but in the final analysis the addition of the quarter window didn't detract too

Starlight coupé for 1947 takes shape with this 1945 clay model.

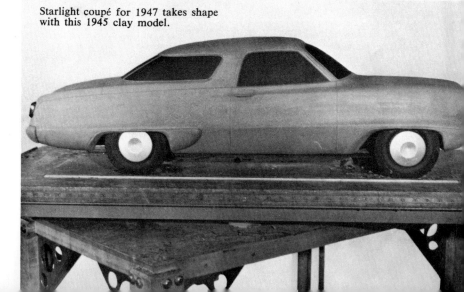

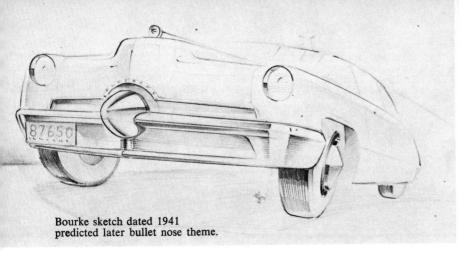

Bourke sketch dated 1941
predicted later bullet nose theme.

Bob created frontal design
on this prototype but rub-rail is air-brushed on.

much from the car.

Another new concept was the reverse-angle slant at the taillight termination of the rear fenders, which in retrospect I must have adopted from some aircraft ideas. At the time I greatly admired the contours of the Lockheed Constellation's fuselage — one of the most interesting shapes in aircraft of the day. The front fender with its subtle nose-down appearance reflected in part the shape of the Connie's fuselage, the bumper guards at the rear were literally an extension of the rear fender contour, with taillights embedded deep inside. The rear bumper was a continuation of the deck lid contour, wrapped cleanly around and under the car.

The clay model at this stage was completed before Mr. Loewy saw it. Prior to R.L.'s return, Mr. Vance would come over once in a while or would call me up to ask about the car. He'd pose a few questions, but would never tell me anything further. He would just say, "Well, Bob, watch the costs." Of course, this inspired me that much more; if Vance was concerned with costs it meant that he was considering my car for more than just a display item.

When Raymond Loewy returned from Paris — he would normally spend about two or three days every two weeks at South Bend — he reviewed the full-size prototype and chose the left side of the model. No doubt he then pro-

ceeded to work out in his inimitable way a plan to sell the idea to management for a production version.

The word broke one morning when I came to work. One of the watchmen mentioned that I'd missed a big show the night before. "Vance and a bunch of brass were here last night," he said. "They brought over some of the board of directors." Neither Loewy nor I were told about it, but that visit must have been the crux of the decision, for shortly thereafter we were visited again by the board. After their second review we were told that the car was scheduled for production!

A rumor has persisted that the board of directors had no knowledge of the Starliner, as it was named, until they had approved a more conventional line of 1953 cars at a meeting with Raymond Loewy. R.L., so the story goes, told them not to leave and suddenly whipped out models of the coupé, changing their minds on the spot. This was not the case, as Mr. Vance and others on the board knew of the prototype practically from its conception through evening visits to the design department. Mr. Loewy, however, in the final analysis, sold the idea of putting it into production.

The road from show model to production car, as any designer will tell you, is not a smooth one. Many things can happen along the way to completely alter

Studebaker clay modelers were "among the best around."

Spinner nose design first entered clay model stage around 1947.

"Mr. Loewy liked the baubles."

Bourke constantly fought "traditional" roof curvatures like this.

what the designer originally had in mind. In this case I was extremely lucky, though some things did occur that left me unhappy at the time.

As previously mentioned, on the original design the rear fender termination was capped at the back with a combination taillight bumper guard, uninterrupted from top to bottom. The bumper below the deck lid was contoured as an extension of the body surface, resulting in a nicely shaped and finished underbody appearance. But this functional effect was diminished in the end by a more conventional bumper, which cut through the area and broke the original uninterrupted surfaces. The rear end was given die cast taillight housings and a conventional bumper with a low-tooling-cost stamping below to help cover certain unsightly chassis components.

My own 1954 hardtop, which I still own, was originally a modest facelift prototype for a 1955 model, with very few changes: a cleaned-up deck lid (no handle or nameplates), a clean hood (no ornaments), split grille as per '53-54, but with half-inch square mesh screening in place of the chrome horizontal and vertical bars. Studebaker identity was placed within the framework on the left front grille. The body sides are devoid of ornamentation, it's blue-black and rides on chrome cross-spoked Dayton knock-off wire wheels. I'm slowly restoring it to its original condition, including all these never-produced ideas.

Other changes in the Starliner were made as we neared production, but none were as significant as the ones already mentioned. The slim forward "A" pillars were thickened, not so much for improved strength but because some director thought they *looked* stronger! The door window was shortened in length and separate rear roll-down-type quarter windows were added. But thankfully the height was not raised, and that alone helped make the car nearly as handsome in production as it had started out in clay. Side sculpture remained exactly as I had designed it, but the door opening was made completely vertical, rather than angled back as it was on the clay model. The basic body and fender contours from front to rear received little modification and, with the exception of a small V-8 or "S" emblem, managed to go into production as a clean basic form.

For a while the front end was a problem. We tried several different treatments. Some turned out better than others, but in general the majority of the different designs left much to be desired. We finally settled on one that I had designed: a simple split opening surrounding a floating horizontal bar on each side. For 1954 I added a number of narrow vertical bars for model year distinction and to more rigidly support the horizontal one. There was also a problem with the low hood because of the bulk of Studebaker's V-8 engine. We had to raise the hood line slightly, but we designed an air cleaner that helped us

Engineers were still demanding a two-piece rear window by the wooden model stage. Bob held out.

Bob Bourke's side of the full-size Starliner clay model.

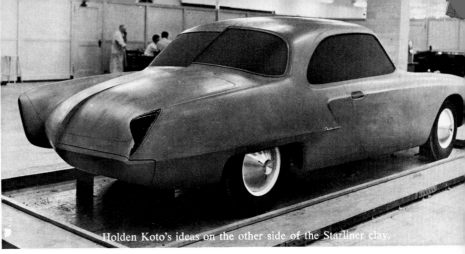

Holden Koto's ideas on the other side of the Starliner clay.

keep it low enough to look right. There was a cooling problem too, the name of the game being to reduce the amount of copper in the radiator to reduce costs, cut the speed of the fan to decrease noise, and open up the front end sheet metal to assure cooling at low speeds. A certain percentage of these criteria were met with an under-front-bumper scoop and a large internal fan shroud. Thanks to Gene Hardig are in order, because without these considerable contributions the graceful shape of the hood would not have remained a reality.

The low-cost way in which the coupé was produced was really quite amazing. The car was designed and engineered with vast economies in tooling and piece costs in mind — this through necessity. Complain as we might — and did — we were well aware of Studebaker's economic situation. After the Starliner was put into production, every component was laid out by Engineering and price tagged to compare with the contemporary Chevrolet. The result of this cost analysis showed that if General Motors had produced this car it could have been built for $385 less than the Chevy! Yet Studebaker sold it at Buick prices. They had to, as their unit costs were much higher than GM's.

We had some weird problems that helped raise those costs. There was one chap in particular in charge of body engineering at the time that I used to go 'round and 'round with because of things he wanted to do to economize. I'm not against cost savings, provided the substitute item performs its required function. One didn't, and caused us to lose over half of our initial orders in the first three months of production.

I was heavily involved with the engineering of the cars, trying to preserve a certain basic mechanical integrity. The aforementioned body engineering man found a door latch manufacturer who would produce a unit for approximately ten cents less per latch than the one we proposed. I said, "Fine, but will it work?" He said it would, and management was absolutely enthralled at the dollar savings, so the cheaper latches were ordered despite my objections. Sure enough, the doors flew open when many cars were in motion, and we had to stop production to correct them. This, combined with a few other more minor problems, created a three to four month delay in filling early orders for the coupés.

Then there was the inherent rust problem with which any Studebaker driver is acquainted. In certain areas of the country, sometimes within a year, the front fenders just ahead of the door would begin to show rust. This was caused by a cowl-to-fender overlap with little or no provision for ventilation or draining. During design stages I endeavored to have engineering achieve breathing space in this area. However, this would have involved additional

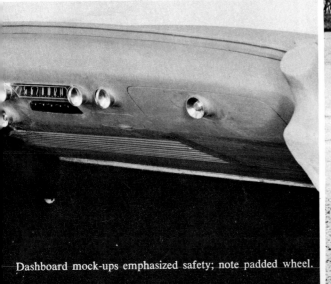

Dashboard mock-ups emphasized safety; note padded wheel.

Final result: despite hassles, it was a great achievement.

Sports car prototype (1955)
predicted basic grille opening of '55 models.

This side of the sedan clay
was fairly close to production.

assembly expense and heaven knows we couldn't have that. The condition, as everyone knows, was never corrected. As a test I changed the left side of my '54 according to my original idea and the fender is still solid after all these years. The right side, of course, is rusted out as usual.

As far as interiors were concerned, I tried to adopt a businesslike cockpit appearance for the Commander, with round cans housing a full set of needle gauges, and a less costly arrangement for the Champion. Both were to be padded, but cost considerations again eliminated that notion. We were very conscious about the dangers of injury in the driver's compartment. The cross section of the instrument panel was designed to increase knee room and recess toggle switches below the rounded top section. The handbrake was on the right side of the steering wheel, not as a "safety factor" as Kaiser were claiming at the same time, but because it was less costly to place it closer to the centerline of the car.

Various interior schemes were tried — door panels with built-in, contoured armrests and recessed door release levers — all too costly for production. A separate front bucket seat was designed for the driver, with adjacent bench for two passengers. In production the seat ended up as a full bench with the seating area accented with contrasting material to give the look of a bucket seat.

Color combinations on most interiors, with the exception of the all-vinyl op-

tions, left much to be desired. Strict cost controls had to be considered when specifying fabrics. This, together with the requisite wearing qualities of the material, resulted in a relatively small range from which to choose. Added to the problem was the directive that window moldings and instrument panels all had to be painted one common color.

The vice-president in charge of sales at the time — Ken Elliott — sent out a directive that specified a mouse gray, the theory being that it would blend best, as it was neutral. I tried so hard to sell him on black I just about died, but he considered it funereal — so all became gray. Although new exterior colors were constantly being developed by us, many of the colors that reached production were incredibly gauche. As I recall, there was a sort of deep salmon that was particularly excruciating.

Then of course we have the sedans. Well, me myself and I designed those too. I was pushing clay, doing engineering drawings, and sometimes I think I was sweeping the floor too. Pretty depressing, right? I did the best I could, but those sedans just happened. Between management and engineering, and the basic design not really being meant for a sedan, they turned out rather uninspiring. Who would deliberately make a car look like that? Who in his right mind would do a rear door like that? Bob Bourke, that's who. I did it all. I confess. I'm responsible.

...tual 1955 result was disastrous plated snout.
Vance, Nance, Hoffman (L to R) liked it.

Large car project was shelved, but greatly
influenced Hawk's grille.

For 1955, Bourke suggested only minor grille/trim changes.

Another rumor I've heard is that the coupé represented our proposal for the whole 1953 line. In reality the coupé began life strictly as a show car; concurrent with it, conventional 1953 cars were being designed full time. The Starliner did impress management though, and ultimately they asked us to design the two- and four-door cars along similar lines.

Hood ornaments played a most important part in the sale of cars, according to Mr. Elliott and his dealers. This was one area of automobile design that we'd use as sort of a release for certain executives. We always had a number of different hood ornaments in process, job keyed with the initials of execs. I'll never forget one of them which was actually offered for sale: "two birds in flight" — or in intercourse as it appeared to me. I understand that dealers peddled them like mad.

Later there was a large sedan in the works, a sort of Buick-like machine which some of the executives felt we just had to have because the Buick was doing so well. Harold Churchill, then vice-president of engineering, said that people in sales and at the top echelon felt the reason for Buick's 1953 success was their massive look and heavy, bright chrome front end. We went to work, but the design was ultimately chopped, again for cost reasons. Still intimidated, management kept insisting on more chrome, and the result was our hamming-up of the 1955 line with that big chromium snout-like grille. It was completely

The 1956 line was Bourke's last contribution. Hawk clay here.

out of context. You readers may think I feel pretty good about those 1953-54 coupés, but I keep remembering these other creations more or less forced on us by the circumstances of the times. Some things I'd rather forget.

There is one point of interest about the '55. Its chromed front end was originally intended to be merely part of a basic painted shell. I had taken the idea from a sports car prototype I'd done earlier, with a forward air intake shaped like the production '55 ended up — but without the chrome and the gliding duck in the middle. The sports car had a mesh grille inserted into the opening and recessed back of the leading edge. But for production, with management clamoring for us to copy Buick, the entire front end was chrome plated — the results of which are well known.

The last thing we did before Mr. Nance dropped the Loewy contract after the Packard merger was the 1956 Hawk series. These were, of course, warmed over from the original 1953 Starliner hardtop and Starlight five-window coupés. While aesthetic improvements over the 1955, they lacked the purity of line of the originals. We came up with the square mesh grille and I kept those little fins at the rear of the Golden Hawk as restrained as I could and still please Sales. We omitted fins completely on the Sky Hawk hardtop and the two five-window coupés, the Flight and Power Hawks. After that the Loewy team departed and Bill Schmidt and Duncan McRae arrived.

Those wild jobs with the huge concave fins were the creations, I think, of Bill. What happened was that the car fell apart from the standpoint of a unified style or idea and became instead a package of clichés which were executed hopefully to promote sales. It was too bad, because some engineering changes had made the Hawks far better cars than the original Starliners had been. But each year they had to add things on, and then they'd try to take things off, adding chrome, subtracting chrome. Then management got into it — and management wives on occasion.

Duncan McRae had quite a bit to do with the first Larks and he's also somewhat known for his line of 1958 Packards. "Dunc" designed the Packard Hawk and others of that genre, but he did so under a lot of direction — rather misdirection — by management and sales personnel. I'm told that the execs kept insisting that Dunc "bring that hood down," until it finally got so low it looked like a catfish. And those *outside* armrests — of all the unfunctional contrivances they have to be the champs — undoubtedly another management notion. One of the biggest headaches for a designer is being credited with such ideas, when at best they're the best he could do with basically senseless requirements laid down by directives.

I was pleasantly surprised in 1962 to find the Starliner design, albeit modified, still being continued as the Gran Turismo Hawk, eleven years after I had conceived it back at the old plant. By then Brooks Stevens had been engaged to make it into a genuine four-seater on a minimal budget. Once again, as with the sedans of 1953, management was trying to make something out of it that was never intended. Brooks had to add that big Thunderbird roof. (He admits it was borrowed from Ford and not the Packard Predictor as Studebaker liked to claim.) He managed to correct a lot of previous errors by deleting those gigantic fins and other tinsel that had accumulated. I assume costs were responsible for the demise of the die-cast grille which was replaced by a stamping.

Yes, it was a lot of fun, and it's certainly heartwarming to see how much one's successes — and mistakes too — are saved and restored and pampered by enthusiasts today. I guess I'm an enthusiast too, because any year now I'll have my own Starliner in shape to join one of those Studebaker Drivers Club homecomings at South Bend. I wonder if that little joint still stands on Lafayette Boulevard. . . ✛

STUDEBAKE
TODAY

The Rude Awakening from an American Dream

One can do more than remember in South Bend now. Exploring the dusty vacant offices, the rickety lofts where pigeons roost, or tiptoeing past the countless silent rows of production machinery that once rumbled and clattered with prosperity, it's all too easy to sense the ghosts of the five generations who labored there. Had some of the decisions been different, would the outcome have been? Probably, but hindsight is cheap and far too easily indulged. One might do worse in suggesting to those manufacturers still with us that they mark the words of George Santayana who warned that those of us who ignore the mistakes of the past will be condemned to relive them.

AVANTI

"I don't believe there's any place in America where you'll find a completely integrated small manufacturing set-up like Avanti Motor Corporation. We have a complete miniaturized automobile factory. There isn't a bolt or washer or nut changed without the same degree of thoroughness you'd find in Detroit. We're making a lot of changes all the time but they're not being made haphazardly — they're tested, engineered. When you think of the size of our organization I think you can appreciate how proud we all are of it, every one of us. We're producing a true craftsmanlike job. Therein lies, in this age of mass production, a unique story."

—Nathan D. Altman, President
Avanti Motor Corporation

Some time ago a few of the "experts" in this business pronounced Nate Altman's Avanti II a dated design. In the same breath they said the Volvo 1800S coupé was pretty old fashioned too — and both Nate and Volvo are crying all the way to the bank. No one has proclaimed VW's Karmann Ghia an antique yet, but everybody knows what they've been saying about the Bug — for nigh onto twenty years.

Point being that automobiles are as old as they look. The Avanti II, at least to our jaundiced eyes, looks about as old as tomorrow. No, a modern designer might *not* come up with a shape like the Karmann Ghia's or the 1800's or the Avanti's, were he to start off with a clean slate today, but such shapes do have character. And they have held up remarkably well considering that today even some three-year-old cars can look positively ancient.

And that *Esquire* story a while back: "For $8000 you can buy a brand-new 1963 Studebaker." Remember? Well, forget it. The Avanti II may look pretty much the same as it did then, but as Uncle Tom McCahill might have said, there's about as much difference as there is between a hank of bailing wire and a greased eel. The Avanti II has been refined, in a great many ways, and detail improvements continue on its slow-moving production line in the tiny factory it calls home. Still, the style and flavor of the original Andrews-Ebstein-Kellogg design is very much with the car, and when all is said and done, it is the styling that evokes all the commotion that Avantis cause. While enjoying the pleasures of the Studebaker Drivers Club 1971 national meet, we spent some time with one of Nate Altman's stallions, and believe us, few bystanders can help taking a good, long look at it. Even in a stolid, four-door sedan town like South Bend, Indiana.

The story of how Nate and his partner Leo Newman, Studebaker-Packard's largest and most successful dealers for the entire existence of that unfortunate alliance, picked up the pieces of Sherwood Egbert's shattered dream and despite all predictions went on to build it in their own plant is ancient history. The wonder of it all is that the end product, a one hundred percent American car, built by Americans and at American component and labor prices, can be the bargain it is for the $8000 or $9000 it costs the buyer. And make no mistake — we think the Avanti II is a real buy. Each car is completely hand built. Honest. Using as much time as it takes, each is custom tailored with the buyer's choice of upholstery and fitments. To say that no two are alike is cliché, but appropriate. Yet it costs less than half of what most similarly manufactured cars cost, and the few that do compete with it in price or quality are all built overseas.

Avanti Motor Corporation expects to reach its production limit — fixed to maintain the quality level — of three hundred units annually sometime soon, and output will be maintained by a vigorous and radically different sales effort which relies on Avanti II owners rather than conventional car salesmen to introduce the mysteries of the car to prospects.

Currently the Avanti II is powered by General Motors' 400-cubic-inch V-8, which to meet emission standards develops a modest 245 bhp at 4400 rpm, breathing through a two-barrel carburetor which has replaced the four-barrel in an effort to reduce a critical fuel starvation problem common to the previous detoxed 350 engines. But the significant feature here is torque: While the 350 offered 360 foot-pounds at 3200 rpm, the new engine yields 390 at only 2400. Coupled to the newly added GM turbo-hydramatic or optional four-speed the sum total makes for a considerable increase in low end performance. New also are an improved heavy duty Dana rear axle and self-adjusting dual servo Bendix hydraulic brakes with front-rear proportioning valve and an improved master cylinder and booster, plus a Saginaw tilt-type steering wheel with collapsible column.

The company has been at work on the option list again. An electric sun roof is now available, and they've licked the design problem of integrating it without removing the built-in roll bar. Every third car is now rolling off the line with this professional installation. Custom-designed Koni shocks — a worthwhile investment for any performance car — are now offered and may become standard, and the Blaupunkt AM-FM radio may now be hooked up to Blaupunkt's equally impressive stereo tape player. And it can all roll on genuine Borrani wire wheels.

These additions do nothing to shorten the Avanti II's production time, which varies from six to nine weeks per car and includes factory tests of all systems, with two hundred miles of road testing over the worst conditions available, all of which help move toward Nate Altman's goal of making each delivered Avanti II as near to perfect as a car can be — something Studebaker was conspicuously unable to guarantee with their own version. To be fair, though, the old Avanti was a production car sold by the usual run of dealers.

Which brings us to the sales situation. Avanti Motors is establishing a new program for what Nate Altman calls "sales affiliates" — owners, presumably satisfied, of Avanti II's who are sent the names of interested prospects garnered by company advertising, and who agree to contact them and demonstrate their

personal car in return for a commission and a discount received when it was purchased. The warranty problem is nil, according to Nate: "We simply pay any Chevrolet dealer to make any repair required under warranty. Then we examine the defective part and if it's a recurrent difficulty, take steps to prevent similar failures again."

Any summary of what the Avanti II is like on the road has to be preceded by a description of its contrasts with the original, which a friend of ours, formerly with Studebaker, refers to as "the world's first droopsnoot, duck-back sport car." The most noticeable exterior difference on the Avanti II — the more level, less nose-down attitude as contrasted to the Studebaker versions — points up a very basic difference in approach. Nate explains: "Buyers of the original were a younger crowd who favored the very low front end rake — and the most sporting exhaust tone. The people who are buying our cars — doctors, lawyers and the like — favor the more leveled off silhouette. Personally I agree with them although it's a moot point because the height of the Chevy engines required that we make the change anyway. I never really minded the rake, but it caused the rear end to lay the suspension bare, and I never cared to see the bits and pieces showing in the rear."

The Avanti II, then, is a sporty car of the boulevardier variety. But that doesn't mean it's a slouch. Ours had the commonly ordered automatic transmission, and we found ourselves wishing it was the four-speed, for the car certainly liked to go.

It was rock steady on high speed bends — something the optional Konis should only amplify — and it took some fancy rod-freak pedal stomping at full lock to make it do anything remotely unnerving. At this juncture it lifted a wheel — or two — and waltzed around a bit out of shape, but we forced ourselves to remember that we were running the conventional Firestone F-78 belted tires instead of the optional radials. Exhaust noise is more hushed with less of the throaty roar that characterized the original. This again follows the concept of a more civilized chariot for a clientele ten to twenty years older on average than those who bought the first Avanti.

Inside the cockpit quality and workmanship are apparent. Our 25,000-mile example exhibited no rattles and the low beltline kept us informed as to happenings in adjacent spaces. It's not a particularly small car, but it never made us feel lost at sea, the way most domestic cars in this price league can. It was all there, sort of hugging us, anchored firmly to the road and eager to do anything one asked of it within the confines of fast, safe touring. No racer is this, and there's no racing potential. None was intended.

Aesthetically there are a few items that cloy, and given the nature of the Avanti II operation we wonder why they weren't caught long ago. Simulated woodwork is almost forgivable these days, if it's well simulated, but the II's isn't. The comprehensive instruments are proper white on black all right, but they are equipped with boy racer day-glo needles and edged with cheap-looking stainless steel bezels that might have come from J. C. Whitney. The seats, magnificently upholstered in anything from Raphael vinyl to decorator fabrics, top grain leather or even Spanish suede, are without rake adjustment — unexpected in a car of this caliber — and the padding around the dash is not too well applied nor of a particularly lush-looking material. As it would appear possible, given the hand-built nature of the beast, we'd certainly try to have these details altered were we ordering our own car.

But! The basic layout of the instruments and controls is magnificent. All are within easy reach with well-lighted labels for the dark. They may prevent confusion in their symmetry at first, but we never could see the objection to symmetrical layouts considering that the owner is going to spend thousands of miles with them and will get used to them in a week or two. Our only complaint about the controls were the overhead rocker switches for the lights, which are uniquely hard to read or judge the position of. Neither were we much for the little vestigial sun visors that do not pivot to the side and are next to useless.

These are trifling complaints, to be sure, and they may be largely laid at the feet of the original design. If there is cause to fault the Avanti II it is precisely here, because with all their care and thought the company has not managed to correct these basic inconveniences, or perhaps simply could not afford to. They have improved most of the material and workmanship to an enormous degree, but they have not altered *all* the original concepts. Fortunately the sum total remains overwhelmingly positive. The Avanti II is a delight, and strikes us as just the thing for the classic car enthusiast who admires American cars of the past for the integrity and style with which they were built — because here's one American car that is still built that way. And as the car's designer, Bob Andrews, who is now — happily — Avanti Motors' Detroit area sales affiliate, remarked during the South Bend meet, "If you can't catch the birds with this one I guess you have no hope."

But the Avanti II is vastly more than a pretty toy. It's a truly fine car, thoroughly delightful to drive, a competent road performer and as dramatic looking and *safe* an American car as you can find. It contrasts sharply with the old Studebaker Avanti — an engine offering performance in keeping with its weight, doors that don't leak, better standards of trim and finish, enough options and interior choices to satisfy even the most eccentric are all favorable. True, you can buy two pretty fine original or restored Studebaker Avantis for the price of an Avanti II, and one can't help but be nostalgic about those old rakish hellions with which Sherwood Egbert once baited the South Bend constabulary en route to and from the office. But like it or not, they're gone. In their place is something far superior, car for car, the kind of automobile we wish the Avanti had been from the beginning: a four-place grand luxe carriage, capable of carrying its passengers in distinct style and comfort for long distances.

280   Quickly.

—*Richard M. Langworth*

Living Legends:
Bugatti Type 41
La Royale

"*If I succeed in achieving what I am looking for it will certainly be a car, and a piece of machinery, above any criticism.*"

Such were the thoughts of Ettore Bugatti as he wrote to his aviator friend Gabriel Espanet in 1913, though in fact thirteen more years would pass before he got around to building it. It was, of course, to become his fabulous Type 41, *La Royale,* the most uncompromisingly splendid automobile the world has ever seen.

Both the man and the company underwent considerable change during those thirteen years. Ettore's innate engineering talent had developed a finer edge. The curious banana-shaped cam followers had been dropped, for instance, and his knowledge of the unique problems of large displacement engines had been increased by his involvement in the design of aero engines for France (though they were produced only briefly in the U.S.A.) during World War I. By the mid-Twenties also his *atelier* was growing from a prospering country business into one of the most respected and powerful forces in European racing. The immortal Type 35, along with the 37 and 39, had by now begun to establish their extraordinary record of victories, and the entire motoring world was beginning to regard this little Alsatian fiefdom and its autocratic Italian ruler with open amazement. Naturally, they were to be amazed still further.

So it was from an altogether broader and more secure base that Ettore Bugatti finally set out to create the world's most magnificent automobile. *Le Patron* liked in-line engines, and eight-cylinder in-line engines most of all. Even with his sixteen-cylinder designs—two for aircraft, two for cars —he scrupulously avoided a V-configuration, mounting instead two eight-cylinder blocks side by side and gearing them together within their common crankcase. Given this predisposition to in-line eights, it's no surprise then that his proposed super-car would also be so powered. What was somewhat startling was the size of it: At 125 x 150 mm the prototype displaced nearly fifteen liters or over 898 cubic inches—two to three times the size of most American engines, or anybody else's for that matter.

His objective, of course, was an abundance of power, perhaps as much as 300 bhp, but it was to be delivered with a degree of smoothness and absence of mechanical fuss that had been previously unknown from engines of that output. The inevitable result then was a power unit of vast displacement which was to turn at no more than 2000-2500 rpm.

This huge engine was also interesting in other ways. The water jackets surrounding the cylinders reached down around the nine main bearings, a possible hedge against failure at that location which had been a sadly noticeable feature of his aero engine designs. As with all his cars since before World War I, the cylinder head was not detachable, which was great for cooling and smooth porting but required the removal and disassembly of the entire engine if the top end needed any attention.

The wheelbase of the prototype, at about 180 inches, was a bit longer than on the five chassis that followed it, which are ten inches shorter. To maintain proper proportions, the wheels (beautiful things themselves, by the way, with integrally cast brake drums carrying vanes around their periphery which draw cooling air through each brake as they rotate) were twenty-four inches of flawlessly cast and machined aluminum. Tires, which were originally supplied by the British firms of Rapson and Dunlop, have been something of a problem for Royale owners ever since. A 36x6.75 cover is not easy to come by nowadays, one of the few sources being the manufacturers who supply the military with tires for gun carriages.

The frame is about what one would expect. Its dimensions are impressive, of course, but for all its massive size it retains the elegant taper of all Bugatti frames, and in fact from a distance it seems almost spindly. Rest assured it is not. Close up one can plainly see that it's ten inches deep at maximum and looks like a frame for a locomotive.

The first car was more or less complete by the spring of 1927, at which time W. F. Bradley of *The Autocar* visited Molsheim and Ettore took him for a ride in it. Though he was already prepared to be impressed (he had visited the factory the year before to observe its progress), after Ettore had finished flinging the gigantic machine around "narrow, twisty, hilly lanes," Bradley observed that, "To use a hackneyed expression, the car ran as on rails, with the difference that it was much more steady than anything on rails we have ever ridden in."

Though of awesome dimensions the car at that early stage was not terribly attractive; Bugatti, understandably, had been unable to control his impatience to drive the car and was not at all inclined to wait for several months while a coachbuilt body was being made for it. So he removed the touring body from a Packard which he had bought a few months before "to see what it was made of," and had it refitted onto the Type 41. (This chassis would eventually be mounted with five different bodies, more about which presently.)

For several months Bugatti drove the car about Europe, visiting Switzerland and northern Italy and attending the 1927 Spanish Grand Prix at San Sebastian in Spain. Contemporary accounts seem to indicate that he was hugely pleased with it, one of which has W. F. Bradley hanging onto the side of the car as Ettore demonstrated its speed and handling and exclaiming, in English, "Good car, eh? Good car!"

If Ettore had planned to sell these remarkable automobiles to crowned heads of Europe only, as some say he did—hence the sobriquet, *La Royale* —it was one of the few objectives he had for the car which was never met. No royal personage ever owned a Type 41, though King Carol of Roumania is supposed to have ordered a bullet-proof one (chassis 41111), but it was never delivered. (That particular car spent the war years hidden from the Germans in Paris, and is featured at the end of this article.)

Still another of his plans never to be realized was an initial production run of twenty-five cars. It appears that only six were actually built. Rumor persists that there may have been a seventh chassis, but its existence has never been established.

How could it possibly be that such a towering automotive idea, so exquisitely executed, was destined to become a commercial flop? Some of the usual answers are probably valid; the international economic depression following the American stock market crash in 1929 and the rapid disappearance of established wealth in Europe. Added to these may have been the natural inclination of European royalty to favor the products of their own domestic manufacturers, and of course, the staggering cost of a coachbuilt Royale—three times that of a Phantom II Rolls Royce, or in today's diminished currency something over $85,000.

The commercial failure of the Royale, or rather the public's failure to respond to it, must certainly have been a bitter disappointment to one of Ettore's artistic, sensitive temperament. He had, after all, spared absolutely nothing from his considerable creative and financial resources in his determination to build the world's most perfect motor car. Above, as he said, any criticism. Well, nothing in this imperfect world is above criticism, but it does seem likely that the Bugatti Royale is the most uncompromised automobile ever made. Given the period in which it was conceived and the development of automotive techniques of that time, there is virtually no way in which the Royale could have been improved—and still have remained a Bugatti. It was a car that, probably, no one else would have even dreamed of building. But Ettore Bugatti was an artist first and last, and artists are not always subject to the cramped limitations which mark the boundaries of most men's lives and thoughts. They have a way of reminding us that almost anything is possible, and that we really are better than we think we are. ✥   —*Don Vorderman*

First Version

Second Version

The Roy

Chassis 41100 (Prototype)

Family

Third Version

Fourth Version

Final Version

Paintings by Ted Lodigensky

287

Chassis 41111

First Version

291

Chassis 41131

Chassis 41141

Chassis 41150

Bugatti Royale Impressions

The most extraordinary notions can come to mind as one is about to drive this automotive equivalent of the Sistine Chapel. Is it necessary to be in a state of grace? Does one cross oneself before or after each gear-change? Will the traffic part before it like the Red Sea? Or is it simply one more in the long parade of automobiles that we've driven so we could tell you about them? There's no disputing that one does not approach a Bugatti Royale in the same frame of mind as one would any other car. For indeed there is no other car even remotely like it. In every Bug ever built one can detect traces of the willful, brilliant, resolutely independent personality of its creator. But it blazes forth from every Royale with such intensity that one can almost hear the man speak, "... *une voiture et une pièce de méchanique au-delà' de toute critique* ..."

Of course, the Royale is large—very large—but size ceases to be of much interest as one begins to examine it closely. The sheer refinement and attention to the tiniest detail are, without question, unmatched by any other car ever built. One can search in vain on any of these cars today for an awkward or broken line, a clumsy fitting or an imperfectly finished surface. The Royale could quite properly be regarded as jewelry, the more familiar domain of such decorous qualities as style, taste, flawless workmanship—not to mention cost. But it is obviously much more than jewelry —and it is also far more than a car. It is a gesture of pure genius.

The Royale appearing here, the one supposedly built for King Carol of Roumania, is one of two owned by Harrah's Automobile Collection in Reno, Nevada. Neither car could possibly have a better home. The standard of workmanship, and scholarship, involved in the restoration

and maintenance of the collection's cars could not be higher. *Nothing* is spared in an effort to achieve one-hundred percent accuracy. Which occasionally necessitates the rediscovery of lost arts; for instance, how to renew the exquisite chased finish of the Royale's engine block? One of Harrah's master metal workers simply sat himself down to a workbench and eventually invented the tool, and a technique, that would do the job—perfectly.

But we came to drive this Royale, not to praise it. Though each of Harrah's Type 41's runs beautifully, both they and we preferred that we use the lovely Binder coupé de ville which appears here. Only the tires are something of a problem on this car; they are totally authentic, having been coaxed out of Paris a couple of years ago, but they are also around forty-three years old and far more suited for show than go.

Now the good folk of Reno are pretty hip when it comes to automobiles. Just about everyone even mildly interested in cars who lives there has seen the collection a couple of times, but we have never known any vehicle with such a knack for riveting people to the sidewalk and distracting other motorists. It is one thing to see this great, graceful machine on display in a museum and quite another to encounter all 7250 pounds and twenty feet of it majestically rolling down the road toward you, strange hissings and whirrings emanating from beneath that seven-foot-long hood and those huge, gorgeous wheels turning around *so* slowly. We followed along behind it on the way to our first location for the portrait photography in a small pickup truck with all our camera equipment, but we could have been riding stark naked on a dayglo rhinoceros for all the attention we would have attracted. When a Royale glides past, all else is invisible.

Having finally got the 8 x 10 color photos out of the way we prepared to move on to the location we'd selected for the shots of the car in action. On the way we rode in the back of the Royale, on that very seat that had doubtlessly on occasion supported Ettore's ample bottom. There's room for two well-fed passengers back there—three in a pinch. All around is carefully understated dove grey worsted and French-polished marquetry.

Roll up those one-half-inch-thick toughened glass bullet-proof windows —one on each side ahead of you and one in each door and the quiet inside is truly impressive. Under way all that can be heard is a deep, distant hum from the engine and the whine of the indirect gears. In direct drive—second gear on the Royale and the one which Bugatti recommended be used for all but the highest speeds—the gear whine disappears and the car is as quiet as any car we have ever ridden in. There is no trace of road noise and you can't hear the suspension working, though it surely is. Compared with the tranquil hush in second the two indirects could be called intrusive. But you don't really have to use them.

Up behind the wheel it's another story—it could almost be another car. Along each side of the hood are eleven doors to admit and extract air from the engine compartment. They also transmit quite a bit of mechanical noise. The Royale's is not a quiet engine. At the top end it is essentially a scaled-up version of their single cam racing eights and, of course, nobody cared a damn how much noise *they* made. But, as we have already said, back in the passenger compartment it is as quiet as a cathedral, and that's where it counts.

One sits close to the wheel, of course, but it's not too cramped. To the far right of the steering column there are two ivory-tipped levers for spark and throttle. Clustered about the column itself are three ivory knobs for adjusting the idle jet, the high-speed jet and idle speed. To the left are five more ivory knobs which activate the car's various lighting systems. Just as all those countless articles have said, there's a horn button underneath the wheel rim where each of the spokes join it. Forward visibility couldn't be much better, but a backward look, and particularly while reversing, requires some considerable neck stretching and head turning. The pedals, typically Bugatti with the accelerator in the center, have easy, positive throws and require no special treatment.

To start the engine you switch the ignition on, turning the key to the right and then pressing it inward. A brief moment of grinding and it comes to life, idling very smoothly at about 300 rpm. Here's still another shift pattern that's new to us:

Providing one can remember it, the changes can be rung with the greatest of ease. The long gear lever is quite stiff in its movements but it knows

exactly where to go, and if you declutch going up and coming down the shifts can be dead quiet.

Acceleration is a sedate, gradual process that would never distress a dowager, although it might frustrate an enthusiast. We figure 0 to 60 should take fourteen to sixteen seconds, but once up to that speed the ride smooths out and the car comes into its own. This is where the Royale is really in its element, and in its time we doubt that any other car could have offered the same sense of security, style and quiet that this car possesses. But then one would expect something more than pretty coach-work for the equivalent of eighty-five grand.

The car moves off very smoothly—this is a particularly nice clutch—and under way one does have the tendency to stay in second most of the time, just to avoid the groaning of the overdrive top. This gear produces an easy 60 mph without any fuss, the next one up being good for maybe 90, so we have profound doubts about the Royale's ability to reach the speeds that certain writers have it credited with—some claiming as much as 125 mph. It's highly doubtful that anyone will ever open a Royale up simply to "see what she'll do." There's simply too much at stake, too much to lose, to engage in such foolishness. So regarding the Type 41's top speed, let us close the discussion with a comment from the factory, which late in 1933 was trying to interest Prince Mohamed Abdel Said in a Royale. "The car," they said, "can attain any speed desired by the designer."

The brakes are quite good, we think, considering that they are without any servo assist whatsoever, vacuum or mechanical. They are of the cable-operated mechanical variety, like so many other Bugs, but can stop all 7250 pounds with satisfying authority.

The handling of the Royale is about what one would expect from a three and a half ton car with solid axles and a wheelbase of more than fourteen feet. It definitely does not dart hither and yon. Changes in direction require a generous amount of sawing at the wheel, taken in rapid small bites as there's not enough elbow room to get a good cut at it. With four and a quarter turns lock to lock a driver would need more arms than Vishnu to get the car safely over a fast winding road. But it is, we think, rather ridiculous to assume that a Bugatti Royale would be driven in that manner.

Haste was never a fitting companion to grace or elegance. And the Royale is, surely, the most elegant automobile ever made.—D.L.M.V.

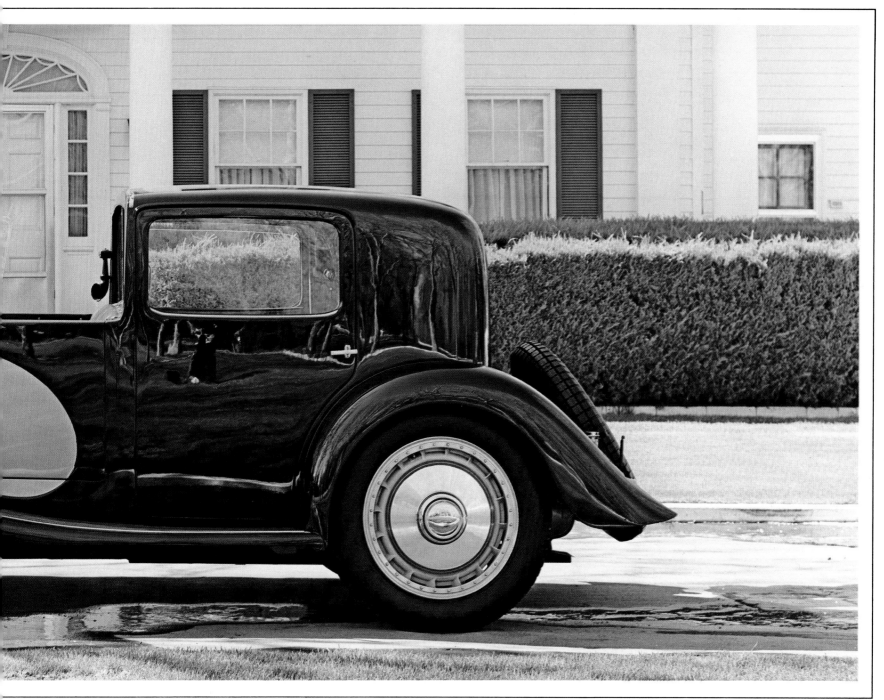

*"Alors, Pierre, maintenant
a la villa de Madame la Comtesse
et ensuite au Grand Casino."*

41100

Prototype

Bore x Stroke, 125mm x 150mm
Displacement, 14,725cc
Wheelbase, 180 inches

COMPLETED EARLY IN 1927

First fitted with a body from a Packard touring car, then a small and rather unattractive coupé, followed by a large, four-door sedan—finally a Weymann two-door coupé was built for it which won a number of concours. The Weymann was wrecked by Ettore and rebuilt as a coupé de ville by Henri Binder. It presently is owned by the Alsatian Bugatti collector, Fritz Schlumpf.

Production

Bore x Stroke, 125mm x 130mm
Displacement, 12,760cc
Wheelbase, 170 inches

The Royale Family

41111

COMPLETED IN 1931-1932

Jean Bugatti first demonstrated his exceptional gifts as a designer when he prepared the sketches for this beautiful roadster which were translated into metal by Binder. The car was commissioned by M. Armand Esders of Paris, who requested that the car not be fitted with lights as he never drove after dark. The car was later rebodied by Binder into another coupé de ville, possibly for King Carol of Roumania. It is now in Harrah's Automobile Collection.

41121

COMPLETED IN 1931

In 1930 a German physician, Dr. Joseph Fuchs, commissioned the Munich coachbuilder Ludwig Weinberger to build a cabriolet on this chassis. He brought the car to the United States in 1937, where it remained during the war. In 1943 it was rescued from a New York scrapyard by Charles A. Chayne, a vice-president of General Motors. The cracked cylinder block was repaired, and the car was restored in 1946. It is now at the Henry Ford Museum in Dearborn, Michigan.

41131

COMPLETED IN 1933

In 1932 Captain Cuthbert Foster ordered this, the last chassis to be privately sold. The London firm of Park Ward was instructed to fit a formal saloon upon it, which was completed in 1933. It was purchased by Jack Lemon Burton in 1942, who kept it for sixteen years before selling it to the American collector, John W. Shakespeare. The car is now back in France, in the Schlumpf Collection.

41141

COMPLETED IN 1931

This chassis was first shown at the Paris Salon of 1932, graced by a well proportioned two-door Kellner coupé. It remained in the possession of the Bugatti family for many years, eventually joining the Briggs Cunningham collection at Costa Mesa, California in 1950. One cannot help but wonder why Ettore, on his own personal car, chose to omit both speedometer and fuel gauge.

41150

COMPLETED IN 1931

This is the one Royale chassis about which there can be some uncertainty. The radiator shell is of the earliest type—minus the gentle flutes which appear on the later cars—so it could possibly have carried one or more of those bodies usually ascribed to the prototype. The car was bought from the family of *Le Patron* by the Chicago collector D. Cameron Peck in 1950, and, after changing hands several more times it was purchased by Harrah's Automobile Collection in 1966.

The next time you swing onto a new segment of interstate highway, accelerating to the sedative seventy that passes for motoring on that bland product extruded by the Highway Trust, it may help to pass the time by speculating on what lies before you. Ahead, as near as the 1980's, is the automatic highway. On it, your power steering is locked onto a guidance stripe and you are naturally encouraged to keep your hands _off_ the wheel. No accelerator need be pressed; your propulsion system is governed by what a smart little computer decides is best. No brakes need be touched, for a solid-state radar scans ahead, keeping your closing rates under surveillance. You _can_ attend to the soft beeping and small green lights that inform you that all systems are GO. Although it will probably be illegal, you will almost certainly want to take a nap.

If this vision of passivity palls, you may prefer to recollect the road a few decades behind us. Here you are not sheltered from but enveloped by wind, vibration and noise. A series of man-machine control loops demand your unceasing attention. You are kept busy warily assessing the radius of a curve, the steepness of a grade, the varying sight distance and the mild mulishness of a steering gear that, unattended, will spirit you toward the ditch. Some modest physical effort is required, and after 200 miles your face will feel windburned, your wrists comfortably tired.

Perhaps you have chosen to install yourself in a Peerless or Cunningham, in a Marmon or Stearns-Knight, or in an Oakland or Wolverine. Perhaps its semi-elliptic springs are disciplined by Lovejoy shock absorbers, Watson stabilators, Gabriel snubbers or even great Westinghouse hydraulics, as grand and vertical as the columns at Luxor. The Kelly-Springfields use Schrader valves to retain their 50-lb. pressures. A set of Weed chains, useful in mudholes as well as snow, are prudently stored in the toolbox, bagged against rattling; and here the axle jack also reposes, wrapped like a mummy for the same reason. Opaline or Oilzum splashes within the iron engine and a Stewart-Warner vacuum tank sips low-octane fuel from the tank out back—where the fuel gauge is also located—and presents it to the side-draft, single-barrel Zenith. Atop the radiator a Boyce Moto-meter provides assurance that you are not presently at a boil and need not adjust the control that tilts the metal blinds before the radiator honeycomb.

The highway you are traveling is as different as possible from the characterless bland ribbon

where this recollective reverie began. It has a strong sense of place. There is a pronounced crown, shaggy shoulders and an average width of eighteen feet, in theory enough to allow oncoming traffic to be encountered with no more than a reflex pulse of alertness. The adequacy of its width is masked, however, by the absence of a continuous center line, which means that you must repeatedly estimate how much the other fellow thinks is his fair share.

Although surveyors and engineers have helped build the road, their services appear to have been of a restricted and almost advisory nature. The road has been laid upon the land, not incised into it, and often follows contours the

way a blanket molds a sleeper. Brisk little discontinuities in its course are found at bridges and railroad underpasses. Periodically you will be held up to wait at a one-way barricade—where the county commissioners have decreed a mile of resurfacing, and where solid-tired, chain-drive dump trucks deposit layers of broken stone, to be compacted by a steam roller and cohered with wonderfully redolent hot tar—and where the arrival of a red flag baton from the far end of the gauntlet means that you may finally proceed, the tarred gravel hissing against your fenders.

Stencilled to roadside telephone poles are occasional state and country route numbers. A

verses by the side of the road

variety of wooden signposts, some with pointing hands, offer directions of varying clarity in styles that change at every county line, conveying a vivid sense of place, and on unfamiliar roads, of strangeness. On your right, behind the fence, a series of six familiar red and white signs unfolds:

HALF A POUND
FOR
HALF A DOLLAR
SPREAD ON THIN
ABOVE THE COLLAR
BURMA-SHAVE

The last Burma-Shave signs were summarily uprooted in the early 1960's. Their numbers had been dwindling for years before then, and their greatest roadside flowering had occurred several decades before. This sets the probable nearer limit of direct recollection at young adults, assuming a tad had progressed from Dick and Jane to brisk sight reading by the age of seven or eight. The farther limit of direct recollection can be fixed with precision: The very first few homemade Burma-Shave signs were implanted in the fall of 1925. The following year $25,000 worth of them blossomed along two-lane highways in Minnesota, Wisconsin and Iowa. By 1929 they marched beside highways from coast to coast.

For four decades these jaunty and impudent commercial messages spiced travel along the American road. They spanned the transition from rippled blacktop to super-elevated concrete, and from Reos and Essexes to Volkswagens and Corvairs. A brief examination of the Burma-Shave phenomenon—which in its strong associative values is often a puzzlement to Europeans—is more than just an exercise in middle-aged sentiment. It is also an uncomfortable demonstration of the depth of the changes in everyday lives that have been effected by the swirling currents of time.

Commercial messages by the side of the road are, of course, as old as commerce. The innkeeper's hanging signboard, with a distinctive name to stick in the memory and a picture for those not facile with words, has been in use for more than half a millenium. For more than a century entrepreneurs have found merit in painting, on prominent boulders and cliffs, admonitions to buy St. Joseph's Oil for the rheumatics—or in adorning barns with rubrics in praise of Bull Durham. By the mid-1920's when Burma-Shave first made the scene, preexisting vertical surfaces such as boulders and barns were not enough, and billboards were already well established along major highways—large, rear-braced structures on which space could be rented to praise The Product. In those preconcerned days we usually allotted only an absentminded distaste to large billboards, except perhaps when in a spasm of avarice they clotted an entire landscape. This may in part have been because they were so forgettable. Usually the message was restricted to a brand name, a slogan and a simplified illustration, this being all that the average viewer was felt capable of absorbing in his few seconds of exposure. The effect, if any, of outdoor display advertising was extremely difficult to measure, though it was accepted as an act of faith as doubtless having a beneficial effect on sales.

Burma-Shave's little signs, initially ten by thirty-six inch pine boards, had an effect that was very easy to quantify. They took a tiny, almost family-kitchen enterprise and singlehandedly transmuted it into a prosperous national company with a $3,000,000 annual gross, one that expanded continuously all through the most prolonged business depression that the country had ever known. Since the signs were virtually the only advertising the company used, and since the enterprise had barely been able to twitch until the signs were employed, they were clearly much involved in its success. This testi-

HINKY DINKY

PARLEY VOO

CHEER UP FACE

THE WAR

IS THRU

Burma-Shave

Rare one-sign California billboard avoided multiple sign tax.   Only the hearty could staff Burma's sign trucks.

monial to the power of advertising was a festering exasperation to advertising men themselves, since several of them had predicted in advance that such signs would be a probable waste of time and money, and the company therefore did without agency services. The little signs were a joyous example of the potential wrong-headedness of experts.

The Burma-Shave story is chiefly that of the Odell family of Minneapolis. While individualistic to the edge of eccentricity, the Odells were people of a sort we have all wonderingly known: hearty, decent, shrewd and with an almost implacable friendliness. It is a personality sometimes identified as "midwestern," being most often encountered in the area of Ohio to Nebraska. It can be partly accounted for by the way of life and heritage of those sections, or even by the possibility that the mountains and salt air on each coast may in fact darken and convolute the native personality. The Odell trait was once skillfully characterized when an Eastern newspaperman described one of them as "a genial, talkative man with a highly suspect hayseed air. 'I'm just a country boy,' he will say disarmingly, but there is something about him that makes a city slicker count his fingers after a handshake."

The beginnings were inconspicuous. Grand-

father Odell had been a lawyer and U.S. marshal in the early days of Minneapolis, but in slack periods he also brewed up and sold, with no great success, a liniment for the aching that he named Burma-Vita. His son Clinton Odell, also an attorney, proved to be a respected and highly effective insurance broker, prospering until a four-year illness laid him low in 1920. As his health slowly returned Clinton Odell, aided by his teen-aged sons Allan and Leonard, explored the marketing possibilities of Burma-Vita. They weren't much. "With a liniment you have to catch a customer who isn't feeling well, and even when you do you only sell him once in a while." Aided by a chemist friend, the Odells invented a brushless shaving cream that had the merit of being regularly consumable in any state of health.

Burma-Shave was no instant success. The young Odells, sent out to sell it by spellbinding individual prospects, often returned discouraged. "If you want to starve to death fast, that's a great way," Leonard Odell observed later. After one particularly depressing selling trip, his brother Allan returned determined to persuade his father to take a flyer in roadside advertising. Perhaps they should try some cheap serial signs of the sort he'd noticed were sometimes put up by gas station owners: GAS & OIL/ FREE AIR/

CLEAN RESTROOMS. "Every time I see those signs I read every one," Allan commented. His father was sufficiently interested to question several advertising men in Minneapolis and was counselled that the idea would almost certainly not pay off. Still, he finally gave the boys $200 with which to try some signs, "maybe to shut us up." They spent most of it on secondhand lumber, some of it from a partly burned building, and hurriedly handmade their signs, racing to get them up before the ground froze in the fall of 1925.

Soon a trickle and then a flow of repeat orders for Burma-Shave—virtually the first the infant firm received—came in from local druggists. The next year the $200 for signs was daringly expanded to $25,000, and a few years later to $200,000! The earliest signs had simply been sales admonitions, "what you might call prose," but it was soon discovered that jaunty little jingles seemed to work better. When the rapidly spreading signs were turned into five-line verses that accurately reflected the family personality—colloquial, shrewd and funny—they boosted Burma-Shave into nationwide success, and themselves became a new addition to the pantheon of American folklore.

The full texts of the surviving jingles—which include everything except that first homemade batch—are fascinating to those who try to comprehend the phenomenon. There was, to begin with, full use of the advertising commandment to promise a benefit: EVERY SHAVER/ NOW CAN SNORE/ SIX MORE MINUTES/ THAN BEFORE/ BY USING/ BURMA-SHAVE. Very soon there appeared an effort to discourage use of competitive products: GIVE THE GUY/ THE TOE OF YOUR BOOT/ WHO TRIES/ TO HAND YOU/ A SUBSTITUTE. There was a recurrent note of almost goofy high spirits, in refreshing contrast to the rancid hard sell then employed in much consumer advertising: DOES YOUR HUSBAND/ MISBEHAVE/ GRUNT AND GRUMBLE/ RANT AND. RAVE/ SHOOT THE BRUTE/ SOME BURMA-SHAVE. Social rewards were suggested, a kind of flirty boy-girl theme that was to become an important element in the canon: HIS FACE/ WAS LOVED/ BY JUST HIS MOTHER/ HE BURMA-SHAVED/ AND NOW—/ OH, BROTHER! A sardonic, deadpan humor, then wholly unknown in advertising but as American as Mark Twain or Artemus Ward, often cropped up: EVERY DAY/ WE DO/ OUR PART/ TO MAKE YOUR FACE/ A WORK OF ART.

Ladies Jump (from fire escapes, to get away from hairy apes) replaces previous set in a remote desert location, 1936.

The Odells were marketers as well as entertainers, deft in their special blend of salesmanship and good spirits. Noting the steady growth of the electric shaver, a threat to the product, Clinton wrote: A SILKY CHEEK/ SHAVED SMOOTH/ AND CLEAN/ IS NOT OBTAINED/ WITH A MOWING MACHINE. Sententious proverbs, which have always ranked high in the folk taste, were delicately parodied: WITHIN THIS VALE/ OF TOIL/ AND SIN/ YOUR HEAD GROWS BALD/ BUT NOT YOUR CHIN. It was soon evident that six signs spaced about a hundred feet apart not only had high readability but also established a controlled reading pace, and artful advantage could be taken in the construction of a jingle to supply a kind of raconteur's snapper at the very end: PITY ALL/ THE MIGHTY CAESARS/ THEY PULLED/ EACH WHISKER OUT/ WITH TWEEZERS.

One special result, rare in the history of advertising, was that people more or less inadvertently committed favorite jingles to memory. Entire family carloads would chant in unison: BENEATH THIS STONE/ LIES ELMER GUSH/ TICKLED TO DEATH/ BY HIS/ SHAVING BRUSH. As with few other commercial messages, the privilege of reading Burma-Shave signs aloud was often a competed-for honor in

the family, with disputes over who might read such special favorites as: SHE KISSED/ THE HAIRBRUSH/ BY MISTAKE/ SHE THOUGHT IT WAS/ HER HUSBAND JAKE. One assignment much prized by small ones, since it took agility and quickness, was reading aloud and reconstructing signs placed for traffic flowing in the opposite direction: OF THEM FOR SEED/ TO LEAVE ONE HALF/ YOU DON'T NEED/ WHISKERS/ WHEN CUTTING.

The best ideas are good in time as well as absolutely so, and Burma-Shave was greatly advantaged by the motoring customs and roads of its day. This was the April spring of the great American love affair with the automobile. It was when the whole family went for a drive just for the fun of it, for a picnic, for a weekend, for a vacation. Cars were personified with affectionate or derisive names, and beautified with a rich variety of add-on fitments: bud vases, spotlights on running-board stanchions, suction-cup ashtrays, extra mirrors with which to detect the motorcycle cop lurking in the blind spot, the first car radios with which to listen—when the vibrator points didn't malevolently weld together—to Fred Allen or Jack Benny, and, after Lindbergh, small diecast propellers that spun gaily in the breeze. It was a time when cars were laboriously

PIGSKIN HERO

COLLEGE CUTIE

BRISTLY KISS

HERO

ZERO

Burma-Shave

simonized, area by area, in a muscle-building program that could take weeks. By the time of Burma-Shave, however, that other major labor of car grooming—polishing off the tarnish on the nickel-plated brightwork—had given way to thrilling stainless alloys and chromium. It was an advance that provided headlights, radiator shells and bumpers that could gleam with a lovely silver-blue brightness after only a gentle rub with a damp chamois.

The roads too grew steadily better: straighter, smoother, wider, although far from the denatured preserves that we now drone along in our current traffic-drainage systems. New earthmovers appeared, including a first generation of "pans"—odd dinosaurs that could trundle briskly and economically along with yards of fill encased in their bellies. Highway designers began to learn several fundamentals, perhaps the hard way: Two-lane roads widened to three invited murderous head-ons, and a divided highway with left-turn openings invited rear-enders that were almost as lethal. Merchants by the thousands discovered motorists by the hundreds of thousands, and on Sunday drives we no longer simply encountered vestigial country stores and diners laconically labelled EAT. A new linear retailing format began to develop on roads near

almost every city. Here you could purchase not just food and fuel but also commodities believed related to a customer on wheels: garden supplies, lumber, lawn furniture, Christmas trees in season and such residential adornments as cast concrete statuary, blue crystal balls and painted gnomes of pronounced charm. These linear retail enterprises were often commercially precarious (wartime gasoline rationing slew them in uncounted numbers) and, since cinder block structures are not biodegradable, their scaly remains can still be seen today along many a dreary mile. What we did not then perceive, perhaps blessedly, was that the linear retailing format was a transitional stage, leading with a natural logic to the huge contemporary shopping center, riding in its great lake of asphalt.

The Odells were attuned to their personal and corporate involvement in the American road, and so it was natural that in 1935 they began using numbers of public service jingles. The first was written by Allan: KEEP WELL/ TO THE RIGHT/ OF THE ONCOMING CAR/ GET YOUR CLOSE SHAVES/ FROM THE HALF-POUND JAR. Anti-billboard ordinances and special billboard taxes increased as the Thirties wore on, and since the company was solely dependent on its roadside signs, the move enhanced the amia-

Maintenance engineer Burdette Booth drove this truck in 1934. Back doors read, ''wake up face, the war is over!''

ble and public spirited image of the company—and besides the name of the product always occupied the last sign of each set. Most of the public service jingles still captured the characteristic tone: IF HUGGING/ ON HIGHWAYS/ IS YOUR SPORT/ TRADE IN YOUR CAR/ FOR A DAVENPORT. Another was among the more beguiling speed admonitions ever directed toward motorists: SLOW DOWN, PA/ SAKES ALIVE/ MA MISSED SIGNS/ FOUR/ AND FIVE. A few moved toward the macabre: DON'T STICK/ YOUR ELBOW/ OUT SO FAR/ IT MIGHT GO HOME/ IN ANOTHER CAR. Others were built around multiple puns: DRINKING DRIVERS/ NOTHING WORSE/ THEY PUT/ THE QUART/ BEFORE THE HEARSE. Most of the safety jingles steered around the more somber overtones of the subject: AROUND/ THE CURVE/ LICKETY-SPLIT/ IT'S A BEAUTIFUL CAR/ WASN'T IT? Some few of the public service jingles which soon amounted to nearly half the total annual crop, reflected the slightly devitalized quality associated with dutiful effort: LET'S MAKE HITLER/ AND HIROHITO/ LOOK AS SICK AS/ OLD BENITO. This one contrasted instructively with a main-line jingle of almost the same period: "AT EASE," SHE SAID/ "MANEUVERS BEGIN/ WHEN YOU GET/ THOSE WHISKERS/ OFF YOUR CHIN."

Analysts of the literary elements of the Burma-Shave verse have posted diverse opinions. The Odells themselves tended to dismiss it as corny, which may or may not have been ritual modesty. George Odell, a son of Allan's wrote a graduate school dissertation of considerable acuity on the topic, pointing out the commercial uses of colloquialism, which tended to make people favorably disposed, even to strangers, or when far from home, and he noted the comic strengths of the whisker.

Some of the jingles were feverish, and others had a schoolyard quality. Many of them could have been considered campy, if the word had been invented in time; in the lexicon of Burma-Shave, preliminary sexual play was "hugging." But more than 600 different jingles were used during the lifetime of the signs and a substantial number of them were very good indeed. It would be hard to beat the fresh allusiveness of: HIS FACE WAS SMOOTH/ AND COOL AS ICE/ AND OH LOUISE!/ HE SMELLED/ SO NICE. Many of the best were fanciful: HENRY THE EIGHTH/ PRINCE OF FRISKERS/ LOST FIVE WIVES/ BUT KEPT/ HIS WHISKERS. Others achieved effective surprise: NO LADY LIKES/ TO DANCE/ OR DINE/ ACCOMPANIED BY/ A

ALEXANDER WOOLLCOTT

My dear Mr. Odell,

Thanks for the tubes. They arrived together with the razor blades which I would not think of using. No double edged blades for me. I always cut my hands putting them into the razor.

Of your roadside jingles I can say this. That I find them the most entertaining advertising copy since "This Spotless Town" verses which were current when I was a small boy. Whether they sell Burma-Shave or not I would not know. I can only testify that they sold it to me.

a. Woolcott

July 11, 1939

To Mr. Allan G. Odell

BOMOSEEN, VERMONT

Early Burma-Shave came in various sizes, all of which elicited significant testimonials (above).

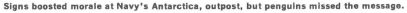

Signs boosted morale at Navy's Antarctica, outpost, but penguins missed the message.

SPRING

HAS SPRUNG

THE GRASS HAS RIZ

WHERE LAST YEAR'S

CARELESS DRIVERS IS

Allan G. Odell and an associate proudly view over 7000 signs pinpointed on their map in the late Forties.

PORCUPINE. Finally there was the lemon flavor very uncommon in advertising: THE ANSWER TO/ A MAIDEN'S/ PRAYER/ IS NOT A CHIN/ OF STUBBY HAIR.

The methods used by Burma-Shave to create its jingles and display its signs were characteristically old-shoe. (It was a company that repeatedly resolved to set up businesslike systems, and that almost immediately slipped back into a comfortably untidy informality.) At first the Odells wrote all the jingles themselves, but after several years the in-house vein threatened to play out and desultory efforts were made to hire staff jingle writers. Finally, beginning in the early Thirties, the problem was permanently solved by conducting an annual jingle contest, with $100 paid for each one used. Clinton Odell served as screener at first, going off to the family's summer place and winnowing out the inept or obscene entries. (Burma-Shave always received a large number of unusably dirty entries, suggesting, if it suggested anything, that even then the public had a continuing difficulty in distinguishing between the dirty and the witty.) Later the screening task became too onerous for Clinton, as annual contests drew as many as 50,000 entries, so other screeners were brought in. When the entries were whittled down to the thousand best, copies were made for all

company officers and directors, and during a week or more of often boisterous conferring and trading, the twenty or twenty-five that would constitute the new crop were chosen. Selection often brought up questions of borderline propriety. LISTEN, BIRDS/ THESE SIGNS COST/ MONEY/ SO ROOST A WHILE/ BUT DON'T/ GET FUNNY was never used, nor was: THE OTHER WOMAN/ IN HIS LIFE/ SAID "GO BACK HOME/ AND SCRATCH/ YOUR WIFE." A third: "MY CHEEK," HE SAID/ "IS SMOOTH/ AS SATIN."/ "GEE," SHE CRIED/ "THAT'S MINE YOU'RE PATTIN'."

During the Minnesota winter next year's signs were painted and shipped out to regional depots. In spring crews of young men, husky enough to dig as many as three dozen three-foot post holes a day, would set forth like medieval almoners and pensioners, traveling for the greater glory of Burma-Shave in one and a half ton trucks gaily painted with such inspirational messages as "Cheer Up, Face, the War Is Over." They would fan out across the country, half a dozen expeditions strong, sometimes on the road for many months, stopping periodically to replenish their stock of signs and to pick up orders and mail from home. They would retrace routes just traveled by an advance man, who checked existing sign sets and negotiated contracts for

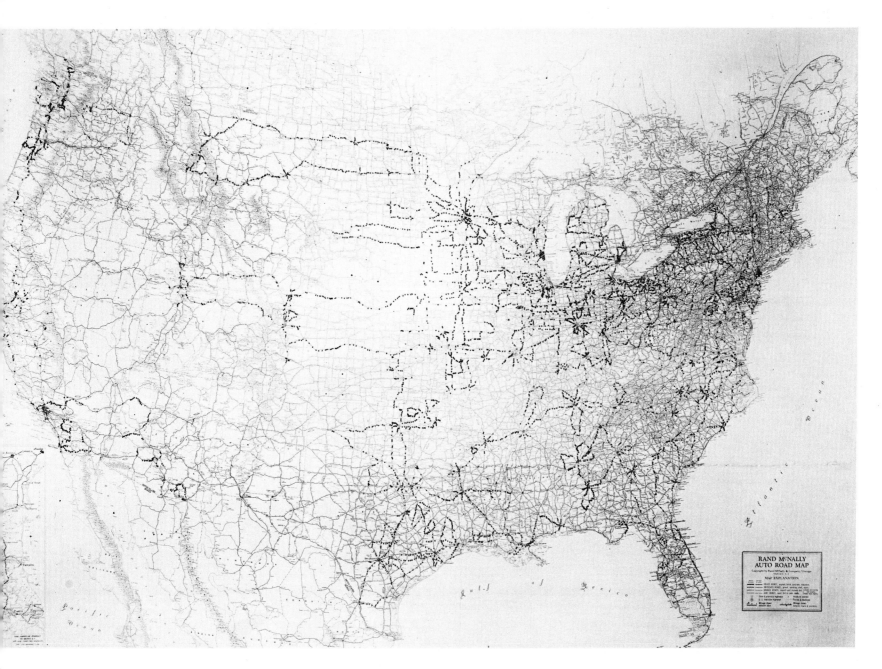

Fanning out from MInneapolis, the Burma-Shave signs were largely confined to the northeast, but were found everywhere from Vancouver to Miami. Can you spot some familiar locations?

Clinton Odell, Jr. (left), grandson of Burma Vita's founder, views silk screen printing process with Burdette Booth.

Allan G. Odell in 1947.

new sites with roadside property owners, typically at rates ranging from five to a hundred dollars a year. The scale of the sign effort was formidable in the great years, with about 40,000 individual signs—nearly 7000 sets—planted in forty-five states. Jingles were changed every year until the task grew too big, and then biennially. The locations were leased at different rates and different expiration periods from thousands of different landowners. The record keeping for all this, with details changing daily, was handled not by a computer but by Allan's secretary for thirty-three years, an utterly unflappable lady named Fidelia Dearlove.

Working the road could be strenuous but it was healthy and varied. Duties were often rotated, so that those weary of travel could often be accommodated in the plant, sign shop or office. Burma-Shave was preeminently the kind of firm where people planning to work for a few months stayed for thirty-five years. It was a relaxed, first-namey place where employees periodically devised elaborate practical jokes for the joyous flummoxing of their own management. Much of the strength of the roadside signs, it now seems clear, derived from the high spirits that, even in times of depression and war, were effectively communicated to the public. Here too

John Kammerer, foreman of sign painting shop.

Burdette Booth, firm's maintenance engineer.

Bill Barber, head mixer of Burma-Vita elixir.

the company was helped by the prevailing standards of advertising of other drugstore products. The contrast was great with advertising for depilatories, gargles, toothpastes and laxatives, most of them merchandised with a repulsive cynicism, in campaigns based on inadequacy, fear, decay, malodorousness and a besetting tendency toward depraved, if not literally criminal, constipation.

Clinton Odell died in 1958 at eighty, having served during most of the good years as an elder statesman in the company. The corporate personality seems mainly to have been formed and maintained by Allan and Leonard. They were the sort of men who had no objection whatever to prospering so long as they had fun at it. Both developed a Barnum-like gift for exploitation. As the firm established its role as a small but unique bit of contemporary Americana, the Odells showed themselves deft at picking up unpaid publicity on national radio and television programs and syndicated wire service features. Typical of dozens of similar exploits was the time when, thanks to the innocent offices of the United States Navy, several sets of Burma-Shave signs were installed in the howling wastes of Antarctica. Nominally they were to sustain the morale of the men stationed at this bleak out-

No wag ignored the immeasurable variations of humor implicit in Burma's idea: from *The New Yorker*, April, 1948.

post, but newspaper readers all across the world saw wire photos of the signs being gravely inspected by a group of penguins. In allusion to the fact that no human female was permitted at the site of Operation Deepfreeze, one of the sets was: USE OUR CREAM/ AND WE BETCHA/ GIRLS WON'T WAIT/ THEY'LL COME/ AND GETCHA.

Inescapably, times change. In the postwar years costs rose sharply and sales leveled off to an uncertain plateau, and then slowly began to slope downward. No single factor was at work. It was not just that roads were wider and cars went faster, although these were elements. Nor was it just that roadside signs went largely unseen by the growing percentage of the population living in cities and high density suburbs, nor that the old custom of taking the family for a Sunday afternoon drive became not just unsophisticated but also uncomfortable. Nor just that the jingles, like the foxtail grown tatty on the antenna, had become aged by the alchemies of taste, nor that the comfortable drugstore had given way to great fluorescent retailing machines that were about as cozy as a computer.

So in 1963, a little fatigued but by no means on the rocks, the company sold out to Philip Morris, Inc., becoming a division of its American Safety Razor Products. On advice of counsel, all roadside signs were meticulously uprooted.

Looking back now, which at present is one of the less troubling directions to glance, it is clear that while the signs may have become obsolete as an advertising mechanism, their basic concept has not. The Odells were conspicuous pioneers in the discovery, now splashed on the nets and the print media, that entertainment is an effective advertising device, one of the best, and that it may actually be more profitable to amuse a prospect than to frighten or insult him. In the late Twenties the Odells began to grow wealthy on a principle that many advertisers discovered anew in the late Sixties. It can be predicted that the idea may be done to tasteless death.

The backward glance also reveals that the signs were genuine Americana, a small, amiable episode in our collective past. This is a perception already made by the Smithsonian Institution, which is preserving one set of signs (Your Head Grows Bald But Not Your Chin) in its cultural history collection. Finally, the little signs have a valuable use today if they serve to remind us that, really not very long ago, we were all pleased to respond to those contagious good spirits by the side of the road.

IF YOU

DON'T KNOW

WHOSE SIGNS

THESE ARE

YOU CAN'T HAVE

DRIVEN VERY FAR

Though it seems odd today, Britain once went without a Grand Prix winner for thirty chilly years.

THE
CONNAUGHT I

"It is not generally realized that most team managers have the option of making their cars seem either fast and fragile, or slow and reliable. It is merely a matter of mystic numbers whispered in the driver's ear."

—RODNEY CLARKE WRITING OF THE 1956 ITALIAN GRAND PRIX IN WHICH RON FLOCKHART'S CONNAUGHT FINISHED THIRD.

British-built Grand Prix cars have won the Manufacturers' World Championship almost every year since its inception in 1958, the exceptions being 1961 and 1964, when the victor was the red of Maranello, and 1969 when the French-built Matra won the Championship. In comparison with the Grand Prix victories scored by British cars since the Vanwall triumph in the European Grand Prix at Aintree in 1957, Connaught's successes look rather pathetic. But Tony Brooks' victory at Syracuse in 1955, when as a, young novice he defeated the might of the Maserati team and sent a thrill of excitement through every British enthusiast, was the turning point in British Grand Prix fortunes. In 1956 came a fourth by Fairman at Silverstone and a third by Flockhart at Monza, and the following year Stuart Lewis-Evans finished fourth at Monaco. Apart from a couple of wins in minor British races, that was the sum total of Connaught's Formula One successes before financial difficulties enforced the team's withdrawal from racing. Yet during the years when the B.R.M. Trust and Tony Vandervell were at loggerheads, when Bourne struggled with the V-16 cars and Acton toyed with expensive Italian machinery, Connaught power rose in a gradual crescendo.

Connaught's strength lay in a combination of three talents: Rodney Clarke, a practical engineer with extensive competition experience with Bugattis; Kenneth McAlpine, a great enthusiast, an amateur Maserati driver and with the money of the McAlpine building concern behind him; and Mike Oliver, the engine development man. Like so many engineers, Clarke's true love was the marque Bugatti; in early postwar days he built up a business tuning and repairing these thoroughbreds; in British Club events he competed with a Type 59 Grand Prix car which he had fitted out in sports trim. Clarke ran his business, Continental Cars, at Send in Surrey. He usually had a good selection of second-hand Bugattis in stock and he was hoping to become an agent for the marque. His works manager was Mike Oliver who originally came to the company as a customer. The failure of Molsheim to re-enter serious production unfortunately brought all Clarke's plans to an abrupt halt.

THE EARLY POSTWAR SPORTS CARS

Rodney Clarke decided that the best answer would be to build his own specialist sports cars. These were given the name Connaught, and although they were based on Lea-Francis components, most of the parts used were modified in some respect. The 1767 cc engine with push-rod operation of the valves, but with twin camshafts mounted high on the cylinder block in accordance with Riley practice, was developed by Mike Oliver in conjunction with Monaco Engineering of Watford — a concern then managed by John Wyer. By using completely new camshafts providing increased lift to the valves and four Amal motorcycle carburetors, Oliver eventually boosted its output to 107 bhp at 5500 rpm — compared with the

ROKE THE ICE

by Anthony Pritchard

70 bhp of the production car. Dry sump lubrication was used with a 2½-gallon oil tank mounted above the passenger's legs.

The chassis was basically similar to that of the Lea-Francis 14 hp sports model and the production car's rigid front axle suspended on leaf springs was retained. However, the independent wishbone and torsion bar front suspension introduced by Lea-Francis for 1950 was incorporated on the "production" versions of the Connaught. The rigid rear axle with semi-elliptic springs persisted throughout the model's life. Transmission was by the usual Lea-Francis gearbox and there was a choice of final drive ratio. Without doubt the most striking feature of the new car was the rather bizarre, perhaps even ugly aluminium body mounted on a tubular steel frame. But this had two major advantages; for its time, its aerodynamics were excellent, and the complete body shell could be removed from the car in under four minutes. Even at this time Clarke had strong views about mechanical accessibility and the whole of the front of the body hinged forward.

Race debut for the new car came at the Bugatti Owners Club meeting at Silverstone in June, 1949, and at the wheel was Kenneth McAlpine, who had become increasingly interested in Clarke's project. During the remainder of that season and throughout 1950 McAlpine and Clarke raced the first two cars in British events — McAlpine at the wheel of the prototype car, MPH 329, while Clarke drove the second car which was registered MPH 996. These chunky, metallic green cars were consistently successful, and they were the direct predecessors of the A-series Formula Two car that first appeared in late 1950, in terms of both mechanical evolution and by their success which encouraged Clarke and McAlpine to greater things.

By today's standards these Connaughts are sluggish, underpowered and with mediocre handling, but there was not much in the way of opposition when they appeared in 1949. Power did not arrive until above 3000 rpm — around 50 mph in top gear — but the engine would rev freely to above 6000 rpm. (Clarke reckoned that the modified "Leaf" unit was safe up to 6500.) Maximum speed was well above 100 mph. At Send Clarke started limited production of the sports car which in this form was known as the L3 and given a price tag of £800 without purchase tax. A few cars were also made as the L3/SR with hairy-looking cycle-wing bodywork by Abbott of Farnham. Production continued on a small scale until 1953, and in all twenty-seven cars were made.

The first two Connaught sports cars at the

THE FIRST FORMULA TWO CAR

When it was decided to build a Formula Two car, Clarke and McAlpine formed a new concern known as Connaught Engineering which at first operated from part of Continental Cars' premises and then, in June, 1951, took over the establishment completely. Formula Two, with maximum capacity limits of 2000 cc unsupercharged and 500 cc supercharged (in practice the latter was never used) had come into force for the 1948 season and at this time the only other British constructor to tackle the Formula seriously was H.W.M. Clarke felt that he had a suitable basis for a Formula Two contender in the Connaught, and although this was a modest enough starting point, he succeeded in designing and developing a car that was a match for its Continental rivals in every respect except power output.

Although the engine was still basically Lea-Francis in concept, Clarke used a new light-alloy cylinder block that weighed ninety pounds less than the cast iron original and had been developed by Laystall Engineering. An important difference was that on the new block there was a gear train between the crankshaft and the camshafts instead of timing chains, and in addition Connaught used their own pattern of connecting rods machined from solid hand forgings. At this stage the engine capacity remained at 1767 cc (75 x 100 mm), four Amal carburetors were retained and there was a separate tuned pipe for each exhaust port merging into twin tailpipes. On alcohol 129 bhp was developed at 6000 rpm when first raced.

Unfortunately this power output was uncompetitive at a time when Ferrari's V-12 Formula Two car was pushing out close to 160 bhp, and to overcome this handicap as much as possible Clarke aimed at keeping the weight of its chassis to the minimum. The frame was based on two longitudinal large-diameter tubular members tapering towards the rear with tubular cross-members and the 3½-gallon oil tank for the dry sump system contained in the main front cross-member. Front and rear Clarke used an independent suspension layout of fabricated steel double wishbones and torsion bars. Another unusual feature of the design — and again one aimed at reducing weight — was the absence of a body frame. The alloy body was supported by its

dford circuit in 1949, driven by McAlpine and Clarke.

own skin strength. In fact this was never regarded as being really satisfactory because it made the bodies very expensive to manufacture, and repair, and an alloy that was strong enough to support itself was difficult to work. The fuel tanks were fitted on each side of the car alongside the cockpit so that weight distribution would not change as the fuel was used up.

For the transmission Clarke chose an Armstrong Siddeley pre-selector four-speed gearbox of the type used in the E.R.A. — mainly because it had ideal ratios — and the "quick-change" final drive unit was a redesign of a special unit developed by Peter Monkhouse for use on a prewar M.G. Magnette. On the first three cars only a limited slip differential was fitted, but this was found to be superfluous. The hubs and brake drums were cast integrally and there were bolt-on cast magnesium wheels of striking design and very low weight. When the first car was completed, it tipped the scales at just under 1200 pounds and was at that time the lightest of all Formula Two cars.

EARLY FORMULA TWO RACING DAYS

By the summer of 1950 the new car was ready for testing, and it was taken to Silverstone where McAlpine hoped to "sort" it thoroughly before its first race. Unfortunately he misjudged a corner, ran off the course and severely damaged the car against a metal post. So it missed its intended debut at the autumn Goodwood meeting and first ran at the Castle Combe circuit in Wiltshire in October. With McAlpine at the wheel the Connaught finished second in an eighteen-mile scratch race for 2500 cc cars to the H.W.M. of Stirling Moss, and later took fifth place in a Formule Libre event.

Already the car had shown great promise, but Clarke was still far from satisfied and over the winter months a number of important modifications were made to the design. Wishbone rear suspension had originally been chosen to keep costs down, but Clarke was not really satisfied that such a system was ideal for use at the rear of the car. So, although the torsion bars were retained, a de Dion rear axle was installed, running above and behind the final drive; lateral movement of the tube was restricted by a compound linkage running from the nearside hub to the chassis frame, and fore and aft movement was controlled by tubular

radius arms on each side of the car. To take brake torque there was a short radius arm and rubber blocks mounted on the differential casing. Girling two-leading shoe brakes replaced the original Lockheeds; and there was a new exhaust system consisting of four short-tail pipes. The carburetors were now housed in what was called a "balance-box" mounted on the right-hand side of the hood with long extensions leading to the ports, as it was found that this system gave better power in the middle of the rev range. Careful development work on the engine had now boosted power output to 140 bhp.

It was intended that the 1951 season should be one of testing and development and the car's appearances were restricted to British races. At the Easter Goodwood meeting the car was driven by both McAlpine and Brian Shawe-Taylor who was usually seen at the wheel of an E.R.A. The car's new suspension was as yet far from fully sorted out and Shawe-Taylor's reports of the Connaughts' bad handling and lack of stability brought it a reputation that it ill deserved. As true as were the driver's comments at the time, by the car's next race — at Boreham — the handling problems had been resolved, and the Connaught's roadholding matched that of any of its rivals. At this meeting McAlpine would have won the Formula Two race had he not by mistake selected neutral at the very last corner! Later in the year the Connaught appeared at Gamston, Ibsley, again at Boreham and finally at Goodwood. At this last meeting, where the car non-started because of crankshaft damage caused by big-end failure, the Connaught had appeared with new and larger fuel tanks which boosted the range from 150 miles to over 200. A few good places had been gained during the season, development was well advanced, and at Send work was progressing steadily on a batch of six of these A-series cars.

SERIOUS FORMULA TWO RACING

By 1952 the Connaught team found itself racing Grand Prix cars and not machinery of a subsidiary formula, for the withdrawal from racing of Alfa Romeo had resulted in all World Championship races, and most other Grands Prix, being held to Formula Two regulations. Mike Oliver had now developed full 1960 cc engines with a bore of 79 mm and these were fitted to the production cars. When the first of the new engines was tested, it was found that with the existing exhaust system there was a loss of some 17 bph in the middle engine range. This was overcome by the introduction of yet another new exhaust system, with cylinders one and four connected to one pipe and the other two cylinders to another pipe and these joined into a single long tailpipe that curved upwards well beyond the rear axle line. Later a similar exhaust system was adopted on the four-cylinder Formula Two Ferrari. On the production cars the wheelbase had been lengthened by one inch to facilitate engine changes. Later in the season the original air intake grille of vertical slats was replaced by a distinctive, slightly bulbous design of the "egg-box" style.

McAlpine continued to race the prototype car, A1, while Ken Downing who had previously raced a Connaught sports car took delivery of A3 and Philip Fotheringham-Parker bought A4. New lead-bronze bearings had been adopted and in practice for the first race of the season at the Easter Goodwood meeting, lack of proper heat dissipation caused big-end failure and the cars had to be withdrawn from the meeting. So the first 1952 appearance of the marque was in the *Daily Express* Trophy race at Silverstone in May. The race was dominated by the team's H.W.M. rivals which took the first two places and the highest placed Connaught finisher was McAlpine in tenth place. The first Continental appearance of the marque came in the Grand Prix des Frontières at Chimay in Belgium on June 1st. Ken Downing led throughout until he eased up on the last lap — his pit misled him as to the extent of his lead — and he was passed by Paul Frère at the wheel of an H.W.M.

The Connaughts were running well in British events and scored many successes in these, but the team's next important race was the British Grand Prix at Silverstone in July. Here a grand total of four cars was entered and in addition to McAlpine and Downing, Dennis Poore appeared at the wheel of Fotheringham-Parker's car and Eric Thompson drove a new car, A5. For this race the cars were fitted with new pistons which raised the compression ratio from 10.5:1 to 12.5:1 and had a much improved shape of crown. In tests prior to the Silverstone race one of the cars was found to develop 155 bhp which was the highest output ever developed by an A-series car running on carburetors.

Although the race was dominated by World Champion Alberto Ascari at the wheel of his works Ferrari, Dennis Poore drove magnificently, holding third place ahead of Piero Taruffi's Ferrari until he spun and then lapping in close company with the Maranello car. The Connaughts still had insufficient fuel capacity to run through a full-length Grand Prix and Poore eventually lost third

place to Mike Hawthorn's Cooper-Bristol as the result of a painfully slow refuelling stop. At the flag, Poore was fourth, Thompson fifth and the other Connaughts finished in ninth and sixteenth places. For the complete team to finish was a fine achievement and the places gained by Poore and Thompson, both of whom were competing in their first World Championship race, were especially pleasing.

Downing ran his Connaught in the Dutch Grand Prix, but retired with loss of oil pressure, and Mike Hawthorn made his only appearance at the wheel of a Connaught when he drove McAlpine's car in a Formula Two race at Turnberry in Scotland. The "Farnham Flyer" went really well and won the race — even though the engine blew up as he crossed the finishing line!

For the Italian Grand Prix the team decided to make an extra special effort and a trio of cars was entered under the name of Connaught Racing Syndicate for McAlpine, Poore and Stirling Moss. The team did the race in style, flying the cars by Bristol Freighter aircraft to Milan airport. The drivers then motored with their mounts the thirty kilometers to the Monza circuit and it was a fine testimony to the oil tightness of the Connaughts that they completed this run without a single mark on their clothing. Although the cars ran well in the race, they lacked the power to challenge the

leaders and success eluded them. McAlpine retired with a broken de Dion tube, Moss was eliminated by a broken pushrod and Poore was in ninth position until he stopped to refuel; after the stop his engine refused to fire and he pushed the car across the line into twelfth place. Connaught rounded off the season by running in a number of British short circuit races and in their last race at Charterhall in Scotland Poore, McAlpine and Oliver took the first three places.

THE LAST YEAR OF FORMULA TWO

The performances of the A-series cars in 1952 encouraged Connaught to run a full team during the coming year and they retained A1 and A7 (a new car that had been exhibited at the London Motor Show) and built another new car, A8. An important development on the works cars was the use of Hilborn-Travers fuel injection, a system manufactured in Los Angeles and used at this time by most Indianapolis contenders. Connaught found the fuel-injection system simple and satisfactory. It gave far less trouble than the Amal carburetors and was far easier to adjust and maintain. The fuel-injected cars could be distinguished by the absence of the "balance-box" on the right-hand side of the hood. At some races in 1953 the works Connaughts also used nitro-methane oxygen-bearing fuel additive and in this form power output

Debut of first of the A-series single seaters at Castle Combe, 1950.   *Engine room of the A-series car.*

was around 165 bhp. The cars raced by private owners continued to be fitted with Amal carburetors. Downing sold A3 which was acquired by Rob Walker, painted his familiar dark blue colors and driven by Tony Rolt. Fotheringham-Parker's car was bought by Belgian bandleader Johnny Claes; it was painted yellow and most of its appearances were on the Continent. The Scottish Ecurie Ecosse team of Le Mans fame bought A5 and Leslie Marr retained A6 of which he had taken delivery towards the end of the 1952 season.

Another new car to be finished in 1953 was AL9 with a longer, seven-foot six-inch wheelbase, and although this was acquired by John Lyons, he soon sold it back to the works. The A-series car in its most highly developed form was AL10 which was not completed until the latter part of the season. Apart from smaller (nine-inch) rear brakes and magnesium zirconium wheels, this car was fitted with a lever on the dash which altered the roll stiffness of the rear suspension and was an experiment with a view to adopting a similar system on the cars built to the new 2500 cc Grand Prix Formula. By lengthening the wheelbase, Clarke had slightly increased the polar moment of inertia and provided more cockpit room. Both of the longer wheelbase cars had re-profiled bodywork and light alloy radiators.

The season started well for the works team and

especially well for the new works driver, Roy Salvadori. After taking second place in the Formula Two race at the Easter Goodwood meeting to Emmanuel de Graffenried's new Maserati, he followed this up with another second place, to Hawthorn's Ferrari, in the *Daily Express* Trophy race at Silverstone. The Connaughts met up with this Ferrari again in the Ulster Trophy race on the Dundrod circuit; Hawthorne was again the victor, but the British cars were out of luck. In his heat Stirling Moss took second place despite the lack of top gear, but a change of gearbox could not be completed before the start of the final and the car did not run. Salvadori retired and McAlpine finished eighth. It was much the same story in the Dutch Grand Prix where Moss finished ninth and last after a pit stop to re-connect a fuel lead, and Salvadori, McAlpine and Claes all retired with engine trouble. Again, in the French Grand Prix at Reims, both works cars driven by Salvadori and Siamese *pilote* "B. Bira" (Prince Birabongse) failed to finish.

In the British race at Silverstone five Connaughts ran, but the sole finisher was Bira who took seventh place. Connaught next ran in the German Grand Prix at the Nürburgring and out of four starters, including Claes, yet again only one finished. McAlpine trailed home in thirteenth place, slowed by a loose radius arm that was caus-

ing excessive rear end oversteer. Connaught missed the Swiss race and next ran abroad in the Italian Grand Prix at Monza. Throughout the race the cars were plagued by mechanical troubles and at times all three cars were in the pits at once. Salvadori retired and although both McAlpine and Jack Fairman were still running at the finish, neither had covered sufficient laps to be classified as a finisher. The team stayed in Italy to run in the Modena Grand Prix held the following weekend. Two of the cars retired and Claes and McAlpine trailed home at the tail of the field in seventh and eighth places. To round off the season Salvadori won the Formula Two race at the September Goodwood meeting.

In many ways the A-series Connaught represented a triumph of development over design, for its modest Lea-Francis origins were hardly the most promising starting point for the evolution of a Grand Prix contender. Throughout their racing career, the Connaught team lacked sufficient financial support, and although the chassis design of the A-series was a match for any of its rivals, the engine was sadly deficient in power and there was neither the money nor the resources available for the design and development of a sophisticated competition engine. Connaught achieved no international success in 1953, but it must be remembered that the cars often retired with overstressed engines, the result of their drivers' enthusiastic efforts to stay with the race leaders whose mounts had some 30 bhp more at their disposal.

While development of the new B-series car for the 2500 cc Grand Prix Formula of 1954 onwards progressed steadily, both the works and private owners continued to race the A-series Connaughts. During 1954 McAlpine appeared at the wheel of a fuel-injection car and Rob Walker fielded a similar ex-works car for Tony Rolt. And these now outdated, but still very active cars provided a fine grounding in single-seater racing for several drivers who later moved on to greater things. Don Beauman, who was killed at the wheel of Sir Jeremy Boles' Connaught in the 1955 Leinster Trophy race, had already gained a place in the works Jaguar team as a result of his experiences with this car. John Risely-Prichard acquired Rob Walker's old car, and both he and Tony Brooks who handled this car on occasions were invited to join the works Aston Martin team. These cars today are still performing well in Historic Racing Car events, and the superbly prepared and very well driven AL10 car of Alan Cottam epitomizes this class of racing at its best.

Goodwood, 1951: Clarke warming up in the paddock.

Later that same day: McAlpine with his foot in it.

At the end of the 1953 season the Connaught team had a vast collection of A-series spares, and they decided to put these to good use by building a couple of 1500 cc sports cars which became known as the ALSR model. The chassis layout followed closely that of the Formula Two car, but the location of the de Dion axle was different; extensions of the rear of the main chassis members splayed outwards and from the ends of these twin parallel radius arms located the axle fore and aft. The cylinder dimensions of the engine were reduced to 75 x 84 mm, giving a capacity of 1484 cc and 115 bhp was developed on pump fuel at 6000 rpm. The bodywork was reminiscent of that of the Aston Martin DB3S. The first car was sold to John Coombs, but he soon transferred the engine to a lighter Lotus chassis; this car was later sold to Peter Bell and raced during the 1955 season by Stirling Moss and Tony Marsh.

A second car was completed during 1954 for McAlpine, but this was rebuilt for the 1955 season. In its later form it had striking aerodynamic bodywork very similar in style to that of the B-series Grand Prix car, but with twin tailfins which were very fashionable at the time. The works Connaught ran in a number of British events during the year before appearing at Le Mans where it was driven by McAlpine and Eric Thompson. At the Sarthe circuit it ran with remarkable speed — it was timed on the Mulsanne straight at 135.47 mph — and with an incredibly loud exhaust note until valve trouble caused its retirement after sixty laps. This car's only other major race was the Tourist Trophy in September, and it was destroyed in the multi-car crash that caused the death of its young driver, Bill Smith.

A GRAND PRIX WINNER

The B-series Grand Prix car represented the acme of Connaught's racing efforts and it was a most ambitious undertaking for a concern of such limited resources. As with the earlier cars, Clarke produced a fairly simple design so that money could be saved where complexity was unnecessary, but at the same time without economizing on essentials. In many respects the design followed that of the earlier Formula Two cars, but there were important innovations. Again there was a simple ladder-type chassis frame consisting of two longitudinal members joined by four cross-members, all these tubes being of 3¾-inch diameter. There was now, however, a light steel tubular superstructure which supported the cowl,

Detail of the A-series front suspension.

With tail removed, showing the de Dion rear.

driving seat and ribs of the body shell. Suspension design was again derived from existing Connaught practice, with unequal-length wishbones at the front and a de Dion rear axle, but the suspension medium now consisted of Armstrong combined coil springs and dampers at the front; at the rear the de Dion tube was located by a compound transverse link and twin radius arms, and there were also Armstrong dampers at that end.

One of the most important differences between the car and its predecessor was that the B-series was fitted with an Alta engine, a completely revised version of that used in the Formula Two H.W.M.'s and in this form made available by Geoffrey Taylor only to Connaught. This four-cylinder engine of 2470 cc (93.5 x 90 mm) featured wet cylinder liners inserted in a single iron casting which was bolted between the light alloy crankcase and the cylinder head which had benefited from development work by Harry Weslake. The crankshaft ran in three main bearings, and there was duplex roller chain drive for the twin overhead camshafts. The two valves per cylinder, inclined at an angle of sixty-eight degrees, were operated through fingers and there were twin plugs per cylinder. When the car first appeared in a demonstration to the press in August, 1954, it was fitted with coil ignition and S.U. fuel injection. By the time the car was raced,

however, fuel injection based on the Hilborn-Travers system was used, but this did not prove entirely satisfactory and from the latter part of 1955 onwards the cars were usually raced with two twin-choke Weber carburetors. Another change made by the time of the car's first race was the installation of twin Lucas magnetos.

As on the earlier cars an Armstrong Siddeley pre-selector gearbox was fitted, and the final drive was similar to that of the A-series. The most striking feature of the new car was its full-width aerodynamic bodywork, an idea evolved completely independently from that of the streamlined Mercedes-Benz W.196 which had appeared shortly before and the Connaught design was far more practical. The aluminium body enclosed the driver to shoulder height and he sat well to the front of the car, with his legs on either side of the engine. The high, forward seating combined with the sloping nose gave the driver excellent visibility both forward and to the sides and was much the same as that of a fighter aircraft. The body was split horizontally along the waistline with the top half lifting off speedily to give access to the engine and chassis. There was a total fuel capacity of fifty-three gallons, with twenty-three gallons in the tank in the tail, seventeen gallons to the left of the driver and thirteen gallons to his right. As the car was originally constructed the dry weight was 1615

After more modifications, at Borham in June, 1952.

After placing fourth in the '52 British GP, Dennis Poore raced at Goodwood, here against Moss' E.R.A.

By 1953 many top amateur drivers had been attracted to Connaught. Above: Tony Rolt. Below: Ian Stewart.

pounds, but by the time the car was raced this had been pared by a hundred pounds or so which gave an all-up starting-line weight with full tanks of around 2100 pounds.

The 1954 B-series car was fitted with Borrani-Rudge wire wheels and drum brakes, but by the following year these had been replaced by Dunlop magnesium-alloy wheels and Dunlop disc brakes with servo assistance — both features being derived from Jaguar D-type practice. The rear brakes were particularly prone to lock up and it seems that this was the cause of both Mike Oliver's crash at Silverstone in 1955 and Reg Parnell's bad accident at the Crystal Palace the following year.

It was estimated that development of the B-series car had cost £15,000 and it was hoped that some of this would be recouped through sales to private owners. To have fielded a team of three cars in major events would have cost £50,000 a season, and for the time being at least Connaught contented themselves with fielding two works cars as and when possible. These were chassis numbers B1 and B2, while Leslie Marr purchased B3. Both Rob Walker and Peter Whitehead ordered cars, and both specified conventional unstreamlined bodywork. Walker took delivery of B4, but Whitehead cancelled his order and for the time being B6 languished at the Connaught works.

RACING THE STREAMLINERS

Race debut for the B-series car came at the 1955 Easter Goodwood meeting and at the wheel was 1953 Le Mans winner Tony Rolt. In the Chichester Cup Formule Libre event Rolt drove a steady, unspectacular race to finish fourth, but the car retired in the Formula One Richmond Trophy race because of broken throttle linkage. By the *Daily Express* Trophy race held at Silverstone the following month two of the new cars were completed and these were driven by McAlpine and Jack Fairman, the latter a test driver of exceptional ability rather than a leading racer. In the opening laps Fairman held third place behind the Maseratis of Salvadori and Collins and on lap six he set a new lap record of 96.67 mph — he subsequently improved on this with a speed of 97.57 mph, but final honors went to Salvadori at 98.48 mph. Alas, Fairman's fine drive with B1 came to an end when the throttle linkage broke again and McAlpine, after delays caused by a broken fuel union, went out with fuel injection trouble.

In 1955 the British Grand Prix was held at Aintree and although only one works car was entered for McAlpine, both Leslie Marr and Rob Walker had taken delivery of their cars at a price of around £5000 and the driving of the latter's was shared by Rolt and Peter Walker. The race was completely Mercedes-dominated and all three Connaughts retired.

After a number of outings in minor races, the next important event for the team was the *Daily Telegraph* Trophy race at Aintree in September. Works streamliners were driven by Reg Parnell and Jack Fairman and Parnell drove a fine race, leading from the fall of the flag until two laps from the finish when the Connaught ran a bearing. Salvadori's Maserati steamed through into the lead and Parnell coasted round and then pushed the car across the line to take sixth place, a lap in arrears. Fairman retired with damaged suspension after spinning into a concrete post.

Later that month there was another British "International," the Gold Cup race at Oulton Park. Although the streamlined bodywork had proved very practical and effective, minor shunts on the track and in the paddock were exceedingly costly to repair and so Clarke decided that the works cars should be rebuilt with conventional bodywork. The first car to be rebuilt was B1 and this was driven by Parnell at Oulton Park, while Fairman handled the streamliner. After a steady race over the Cheshire circuit Parnell finished fourth behind Moss (works Maserati), Hawthorn

Start of a 1½-liter sports car race, Goodwood, 1955, which Les Leston won despite an altercation with a fence.

Below: Leston again, at Silverstone a month later, where he missed another 1½-liter win by twenty-two seconds.

(Ferrari-entered Lancia) and Titterington (Vanwall), but Fairman's car together with the private entries of Peter Walker (with the Rob Walker car) and Leslie Marr all retired.

GRAND PRIX VICTORY AT LAST

Already the Connaught team was finding the financial burden of racing the B-series cars oppressive and was on the verge of withdrawing from racing. Then Connaught received a rather late invitation to run in the Syracuse Grand Prix to be held on October 23rd. The starting money offered — close to a £1000 per car — was irresistible and the team welcomed the opportunity to test the cars in a full-length Continental Grand Prix. At short notice it was difficult to find suitable drivers, but Clarke eventually arranged for young dental student Tony Brooks, who had previously appeared at

the wheel of the works sports car, and Les Leston to drive the cars in the Sicilian race. After only a very brief testing session at Goodwood the Connaughts were loaded into their transporters — converted ex-London "Green Line" coaches — and set off on their 2000-mile trek. In this race the Connaughts faced nine Maseratis — four of them works cars — the Modena attack spear-headed by Luigi Musso and Luigi Villoresi.

To no one's amazement Musso was fastest in practice at 2 minutes 3.8 seconds, but Brooks with the exposed-wheel car soon familiarized himself with the triangular, bumpy 3.4-mile circuit and his best lap of 2 minutes 5.4 seconds put him also on the front row of the starting grid. Leston's car was plagued by fuel-feed trouble and only managed eight laps of practice in all.

The Maseratis of Musso and Villoresi surged in-

to the lead at the start of the race, while Brooks, unaccustomed to moving off with so much power under his throttle foot, almost stalled and made a very slow start. By the end of the first lap Brooks had recovered and was in fourth place with Leston fifth, but a long way back. As the race progressed Brooks gradually began to pick up places, slipping into third place ahead of Schell's streamlined Maserati on lap four, and two laps later he had moved into second place ahead of Villoresi. On eleven, Brooks surged past Musso's leading Maserati, the Italian fought back, re-passing the Connaught and then Brooks went ahead again. The Connaught steadily drew away from the Italian car which was slowed by weakening brakes and gearbox trouble, and at the checkered flag Brooks was fifty-one seconds ahead of Musso and had set a new lap record at 102.3 mph (2 minutes

---

L3 SPORTS CAR, 1950-1953

ENGINE
Capacity: 1767 cc (75 x 100 mm); *No. of cylinders*: 4; *Valve actuation*: twin high-mounted camshafts operating the valves through pushrods; *Valves*: two per cylinder at an inclined angle of 90 degrees; *Carburetion*: four Amal 276 instruments; *Ignition*: Lucas coil; *Lubrication*: dry sump; *Power output*: 107 bhp at 5500 rpm.

TRANSMISSION
Clutch: dry single-plate; *Gearbox*: four-speed with synchromesh on the upper three ratios; *Final drive*: semi-floating spiral bevel.

CHASSIS
Frame: partial box-section side-members with channel-section and tubular cross-members; *Front suspension*: independent by torsion bars and wishbones; *Rear suspension*: rigid axle and semi-elliptic springs; *Steering*: worm and nut; *Brakes*: Girling hydro-mechanical; *Tire size*: 6.00 x 16; *Wheelbase*: 8 feet 3 inches; *Front track*: 4 feet 3½ inches; *Rear track*: 4 feet 4⅜ inches; *Overall length*: 12 feet 3 inches; *Dry weight*: 2100 pounds.

A-SERIES FORMULA TWO CAR, 1952-1953

ENGINE
Capacity: 1960 cc (79 x 100 mm); *No. of cylinders*: 4; *Valve actuation*: twin high-mounted camshafts operating the valves through pushrods; *Valves*: two per cylinder at an included angle of 90 degrees; *Carburetion*: four Amal 10. T.T.9 instruments or Hilborn-Travers fuel injection; *Ignition*: Scintilla N.V.4 magneto driven from the rear of the exhaust camshaft; *Lubrication*: dry sump; *Power output*: approx. 145 bhp at 6000 rpm.

TRANSMISSION
Gearbox: Armstrong Siddeley pre-selector four-speed (clutchless); *Final drive*: lowered shaft driving straight-cut crown wheel and bevel through quick-change spur transfer gears.

CHASSIS
Frame: tubular ladder-type with tubular cross-members; *Front suspension*: independent by fabricated unequal-length wishbones, torsion bars and anti-roll bar; *Rear suspension*: de Dion axle, torsion bars, single radius rods, central torque rod and compound linkage for lateral location; *Steering*: rack and pinion; *Brakes*: Girling hydraulic two-leading shoe, 12 x 2 inch drums (9 inch rear drums on last two cars); *Tire size*: Front — 5.50 x 15, rear — 6.00 x 15; *Wheelbase*: 7 feet 1 inch (7 feet 6 inches on last two cars); *Front track*: 3 feet 10½ inches; *Rear track*: 4 feet 5½ inches; *Overall length*: 12 feet 11 inches; *Dry weight*: 1230/1280 pounds.

B-SERIES GRAND PRIX CAR, 1955-1957

ENGINE
Capacity: 2470 cc (93.5 x 90 mm); *No. of cylinders*: 4; *Valve actuation*: twin overhead camshafts driven by a single long duplex roller chain from the rear of the crankshaft; *Valves*: two per cylinder at an included angle of 72 degrees; *Carburetion*: Hilborn-Travers-type fuel injection early in 1955, but two twin-choke Weber instruments later substituted; *Ignition*: twin Lucas magnetos and twin plugs per cylinder; *Lubrication*: dry sump; *Power output*: 240 bhp at 6400 rpm.

TRANSMISSION
Gearbox: Armstrong Siddeley pre-selector four-speed (clutchless) mounted close to the rear axle; *Final drive*: straight-cut crown wheel and bevel with quick-change spur transfer gears.

CHASSIS
Frame: tubular ladder-type with tubular cross-members; *Front suspension*: tubular, square-section unequal-length wishbones, combined coil spring/damper units and anti-roll bar. *Rear suspension*: de Dion axle, single radius arms, central torque rod and compound linkage for lateral location; *Steering*: rack and pinion; *Brakes*: Dunlop 10.5 inch disc with servo assistance; *Tire size*: front — 4.50 x 16, rear — 5.00 x 16; *Wheelbase*: 7 feet 6 inches; *Front and rear track*: 4 feet 2 inches; *Overall length*: 14 feet 4 inches; *Dry weight*: 1560 pounds.

0.2 seconds). Leston, completely out of luck, was delayed by magneto trouble and after three stops for plug changes, he finished ninth and last, all of eight laps in arrears. For Connaught this was a magnificent and unexpected victory. It was in fact the first important Grand Prix win by a British car since Segrave's victory with a Sunbeam at San Sebastian thirty years before! It provided Connaught with stimulus and encouragement when it was vitally needed and despite their financial worries the team decided to continue racing.

1956: A SEASON OF PERSEVERANCE

So impressed was the Sicilian driver Piero Scotti by the performance of the Connaught at Syracuse that he purchased B6, the car intended for Whitehead, and 1956 witnessed the very odd situation of a British Grand Prix car being raced in Italian red colors. In recognition of the Sicilian success the B-series car now became known as the "Syracuse" model. Another new car, B7, was completed by the start of the season.

The team's first race in 1956 was again at Syracuse. This event had been brought forward to April, its usual place in the calendar, and here Connaughts were driven by Scotti and Desmond Titterington. Neither of the cars could match Brooks' lap speeds of the previous October and both retired. The cars then ran at the Easter Goodwood meeting and after new works driver Archie Scott-Brown had retired with a broken crankshaft (for much of the way he had led the field), the other works cars of Les Leston and Bob Gerard finished third and fourth behind the Maseratis of Moss and Salvadori. Scott-Brown — despite the terrible handicap of an unformed right hand — was an exceptionally quick driver and in the Aintree "200" race later in April he led until his car burnt a piston. Titterington drove a streamlined car in this race and had a lucky escape when he lost his brakes completely and crashed.

The cars next ran in the *Daily Express* Trophy race at Silverstone which was dominated by Stirling Moss at the wheel of the much improved Vanwall. Scott-Brown and Titterington finished second and third for Send, and Scotti drove a steady, cautious race to take seventh place. At this race Mike Oliver had a rare drive, but crashed when his car succumbed to brake trouble. With Rob Walker's car and the works entry for Fairman there were six "Syracuse" models in this race (out of the seven built) together with four of the old Formula Two model. At Silverstone, Scotti's car had been painted red, but when he next drove it, in the Belgian Grand Prix at Spa, it was back in

green. Here the Sicilian retired with loss of oil pressure in the gearbox lubrication system. Ever since Scotti had taken delivery of B6, it had been plagued by teething troubles, and he was now thoroughly dissatisfied with it. He terminated his agreement with the Connaught team, and the car languished at the works once more.

As a result of the difficulties experienced with the Dunlop brakes, by the British Grand Prix at Silverstone one car had been fitted with Girling discs. Scott-Brown, as usual, set the pace for the Connaught team and "mixed it" with the Italian cars until a driveshaft broke; then the steady, plodding Fairman came through to finish fourth behind the Lancia-Ferraris of Fangio and Collins and Behra's Maserati. Connaught could not afford to run in any more major races until September when three cars were fielded in the Italian Grand Prix at Monza. Here Ron Flockhart, deputizing for Scott-Brown who was not allowed to start because of his disability, drove a swift, consistent race to take a fine third place behind Moss's Maserati and Fangio's Lancia-Ferrari. This race was run on the full Monza road and banked track circuit and the bumpy banking took its toll of suspension failures; Fairman with another Connaught crossed the line in fifth place, the front wheels leaning inwards because of the failure of the front cross-member and the bottom of the engine scraping on the ground. This was Connaught's best performance since Syracuse and once again provided the encouragement needed to carry on an uphill struggle.

1957: THE FINAL FLING

Connaught had expended £20,000 on their 1956 racing program, very little success had been gained

Last and fastest of the 1½-liter streamlined two sea[t]

Goodwood, April 1955: Clarke with streamlined GP car.
One month later McAlpine does battle with Ken Wharton's open-wheel Vanwall at Silverstone; both retired.

326

car above was written off during the 1955 T.T.

The GP-winning Syracuse-type car back at Monza in 1956.

Last race of 1955: both Parnell's Connaught and Moss' GP Maserati easily outran the field, then blew up.

in return, and Clarke was well aware that the Alta engine was still not reliable enough and no longer powerful enough to be competitive. It was only now, at the beginning of 1957, with new and stronger connecting rods and modifications to the valves and valve gear that the Alta engine was developing the 240 bhp originally claimed. Several new developments were in hand, but only one of these was raced. This was a body of dart shape with slim, tapering, angular nose and high tail that was built on the chassis of B3 — it was nicknamed the "toothpaste-tube." Work was nearing completion on the new C-series car with space-frame chassis, strut and coil spring front suspension and inboard rear brakes, and Clarke was also working on a D-series rear-engined car. If adequate financing had been available, Connaught would have been a pioneer of the modern rear-engined Grand Prix car, for as long ago as January, 1954, Clarke had released details of a projected rear-engined car to be known as the J3 and powered by the Coventry-Climax V-8 "Godiva" engine that never reached the race track.

In 1957 Connaught's first outing was again at Syracuse, but the race proved a dismal failure. Les Leston was to drive B1, the very first of the series, but in practice the right-hand driveshaft broke, lashed through the fuel tank which ignited and while Leston jumped clear, the blazing car crashed into a wall and was burnt out. Ivor Bueb, co-winner at Le Mans in 1955, finished fifth.

Stuart Lewis-Evans drove the as yet unpainted "dart" in the Richmond Trophy race at Goodwood on Easter Monday and after the retirement of the Vanwalls and Scott-Brown's Connaught won the race from the Rob Walker-owned "Syracuse" driven by Jack Fairman. The same day there was held the Pau Grand Prix and Bueb drove a spirited race to finish third behind a brace of works Maseratis and Leston took fifth place. One car then travelled on to Naples where it was driven by Lewis-Evans. The little Welshman hounded the works Lancia-Ferraris and had moved up to second place ahead of Hawthorn's when a front hub fractured because of a faulty casting. At Monaco two cars were fielded for Lewis-Evans and Bueb, and both of these had special short noses to prevent bodywork damaged in the many bumps and scrapes that characterize this race from blocking off the air-flow to the radiators. Just before the start, the gearbox was damaged on Bueb's car, and he had to drive the practice hack. Lewis-Evans finished fourth with the "dart," but Bueb had a thoroughly miserable race; his car was plagued by innumerable troubles, and he eventually retired with a split fuel tank.

Immediately after Monaco McAlpine and Clarke issued a statement that the team was regretfully withdrawing from racing. The tremendous cost of running a Grand Prix team was proving more than even McAlpine could afford, but the decision was altogether depressing to British motor racing enthusiasts; the new four-cylinder B.R.M.'s were still hopelessly unreliable, and the Vanwalls were only just finding their form. Connaught had achieved more than the combined efforts of these two teams. After their fleeter, but more brittle, rivals had been pushed away into retirement, the Connaughts would still be plodding round and there was usually at least one car in the money at the finish.

In September of 1957 the complete Connaught équipe of cars and equipment was auctioned. Two of the cars — including the "dart"— were bought by Bernard Ecclestone and although he tried to race them during the 1958 season, without any works support or development program it was a hopeless business. The C-series car was eventually completed by Paul Emery, and it was driven in the 1959 United States Grand Prix by Bob Said, but retired after only a single lap. It was brought back to England and rebuilt, and an abortive attempt was then made to qualify it at Indianapolis in 1962.

The days of the wealthy, dedicated amateur like McAlpine are long gone, and it is perhaps a rather sad thing that Grand Prix racing is now a harder, much more commercially orientated sport. Happily, memories of this great era in racing are still roused by the sight and sound of these gallant cars competing at Vintage Sports Car Club meetings. ✤

CONNAUGHT

AL10
still running-and winning

Connaught No. AL10 was the last of the Formula Two cars manufactured by Connaught Engineering. It was built early in 1953, fitted with fuel injection as standard equipment, and, as No. AL9, sported a chassis six inches longer than all the other Formula Two cars. It was raced by the factory during 1953, Kenneth McAlpine, Stirling Moss and Roy Salvadori driving — but without any major success. Some two years later the car was sold to John Coombs, who during the course of his ownership blew the engine and had the car fitted with a brand-new one at the factory,

whereupon it was sold to John Horton of Sutton Coldfield. During the next eight years Mr. Horton maintained the car in completely original condition, only occasionally contesting it in club meetings. In 1964 Alan S. Cottam purchased the car, and in the years that followed has driven it to considerable success in vintage races throughout England.

Recently we wrote to Mr. Cottam asking for more background on AL10. In addition to providing us with its history, he offered these most interesting observations: "When I obtained the car it was basically in sound condition but re-

quired major engine rebuild. We did actually run the vehicle in two events before stripping it, however, in order to find out what the performance and general handling were like. When we stripped the engine all the bearings were replaced but the cylinder head gasket material was changed from the original Connaught specification to one of our own. A milder exhaust camshaft was fitted and also some re-rated valve springs (the valve springs being of a slightly lower poundage). The idea of this was to try and obtain a little more torque on the engine and to relieve some of the

stresses on the valve gear (which had tendency to break cam followers) and also to try and keep the water out of the oil and the oil out of the water — which appeared to be a constant source of trouble when the cars were run by the works. This would appear to have been fairly successful, because in the seven years that I have had it, it has won something in the region of forty to fifty awards, both in circuit racing and hill climbing. The car still holds the record in its class at Prescott, Shelsley Walsh and Curborough and it has won the award for the best front-engined racing car five out of six times and the best unlimited front engined racing car on two occasions.

". . . on a ratio which is suitable for Silverstone and Thruxton the car will pull approximately 120-130 mph in top, 100 mph in third, about 78 mph in second and about 58 mph in first. Generally speaking, the impressions that the car has given me are that as long as one does not take liberties, the road holding is extremely good. The brakes are superb, but in comparison to the E.R.A.'s and Maseratis, the car is underpowered.

"The main reason why I think this car has been successful is solely due to the fact that the engine, which gives approximately 142 hp, develops its power in the right places — and the chassis, being well designed, can use all of it nearly all the time. . . . One of the things I like most of all about it is that I think it is the most beautifully made car that Connaught ever produced and also probably one of the best engineered cars of its era. The only thing which I dislike about the car is that if you do happen to make a mistake then it is extremely difficult to recover."

Judging from Mr. Cottam's growing list of victories, however, he seems to manage very well. ✠

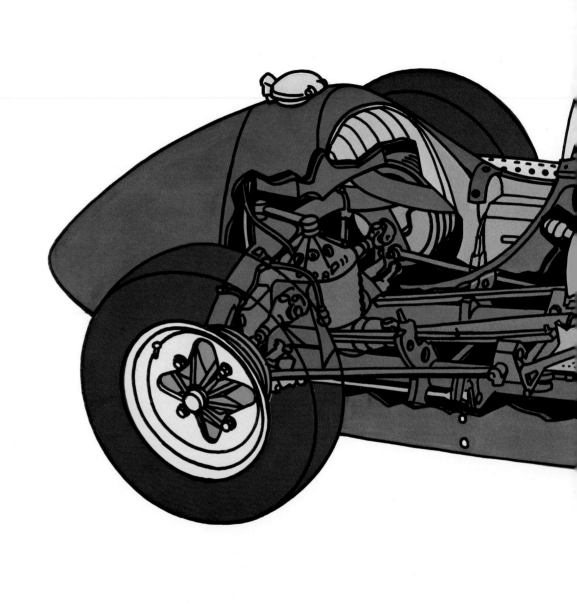

cutaway drawing by Ken Rush

TWO NEW BOOKS
IN OUR LIBRARY SERIES

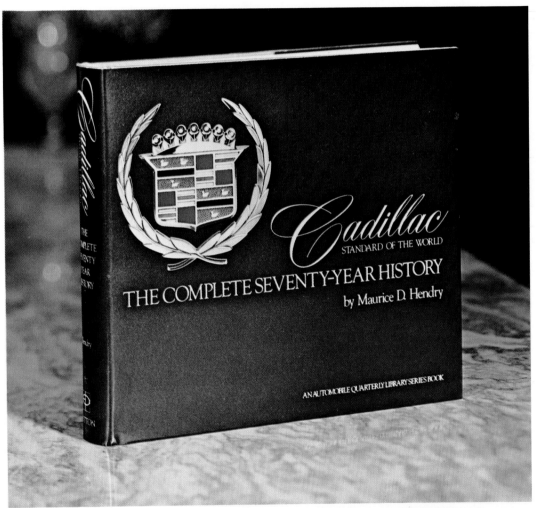

Cadillac
STANDARD OF THE WORLD
THE COMPLETE SEVENTY-YEAR HISTORY
by Maurice D. Hendry

AN AUTOMOBILE QUARTERLY LIBRARY SERIES BOOK

8½ x 9½ INCHES · APPROXIMATELY 400 PAGES
MORE THAN 300 PHOTOGRAPHS
A PORTFOLIO OF 73 CADILLACS (1903 TO DATE) AND LaSALLES—IN FULL COLOR
REGULAR PRICE: $18.95   PRICE TO AQ SUBSCRIBERS: $16.95

Never before has the Cadillac automobile been so comprehensively examined as in this definitive history of the car that set the "Standard of the World." And never before has there been a volume which so lavishly presents between two covers hundreds of photographs pictorially documenting that history.

AUTOMOBILE *Quarterly* contributing editor Maurice D. Hendry weaves the fabric of Cadillac's history through twelve fascinating chapters: Henry Martyn Leland and his apprenticeship in the precision manufacture of armaments in the post Civil War era; the formation of his own firm; his entrance into a company that would bear the name Cadillac; the pacesetting single-cylinder car that would demonstrate the practicability of standardization of parts and win for Cadillac the Dewar Trophy; the introduction of the Cadillac Thirty; a behind-the-scenes look at Cadillac's joining General Motors; the development of the self starter and again the Dewar Trophy; the V-8 engine and the succession of Cadillacs which carried it; the Lelands taking leave of the company and Cadillac's production for World War I; the postwar reorganization and return to peacetime automotive research and development; the Cadillac in service in the sands of the Middle East and cross country in the United States; the development of the V-16 and the V-12 and the fabulous Cadillacs of the classic era; subsequent developments of the Thirties and Cadillac's production for the war effort; the postwar era with Cadillac's high compression ohv V-8 and the irrepressible tailfin; the limited edition Eldorado and the Eldorado Brougham; the DeVille, Calais and front wheel drive Eldorado. Cadillac has packed a lot into its seventy years. Nothing is missed here. And the narrative is spiced by reminiscences of those who were there when it happened, those who made it happen.

Nor is this all! This big book also presents an illuminating (and gorgeous) pictorial album of Cadillacs in the classic years, with commentary by Dave Holls; a special illustrated supplement on the history of LaSalle by Jeffrey I. Godshall; a study of Cadillac heraldry researched by Harry Pulfer; a table researched by William R. Tite delineating — by both model and calendar year — the complete Cadillac production record. Plus much, much more.

For decades the Cadillac automobile has been deserving of a full-scale luxury presentation of its history. This is the book that pays homage.

334

TO ORDER EITHER OF THESE BOOKS,
USE THE ENCLOSED POSTPAID PRINTS & SUBSCRIPTION ENVELOPE.

As this issue proceeded to press, the staff of AUTOMOBILE Quarterly *was putting the finishing touches on two big new books which will be published this fall. Herewith a sneak preview of these books—and an invitation to our subscribers to acquire one or both at substantial savings over the regular price.*

Corvette! Star-spangled it is — and at last here is the first complete story of America's most popular sports car. A virtual feast of historical narrative and fascinating photographs — hundreds of them — that will assuredly satisfy the appetite of every American enthusiast.

AUTOMOBILE *Quarterly* contributing editor Karl Ludvigsen tells the story in eighteen exciting chapters — no one could tell it better — setting the scene with America's rediscovery of the sports car in the early Fifties and Chevrolet's embarking on the adventure; then following the travels of the first Corvette, from the inspirations of Harley Earl and Maurice Olley to its first showing at the GM Motorama; the subsequent decision to build the car, the travails of its launching on the market, the first attempts to race it; Zora Arkus-Duntov's entrance on the scene, the last minute decision to revise the car, not drop it; the Corvette survival by racing in 1956; the Corvette SS and the all-out effort in 1957; the development of fuel injection for the Corvette; the SR-2 and XP-700 racing and show car versions; the flirtation with mid-engined designs; racing at Le Mans in 1960; the Sting Ray racer; the Corvette maturation, 1961-1962; the inside story of the exotic single-seater CERV; the all-new Corvette of 1963, the Year of the Sting Ray; the incredible saga of the five special lightweight Corvettes; the improved Stingray of 1964-1967; the spectacular Mako Shark; the transformation of the Corvette for 1968; the Corvette of the Seventies; and the contemporary mid-engine investigations as well as the Chaparral-related projects.

The Corvette story is as fast-paced as the cars it describes. It's a fascinating look at "The Real McCoy." And the appendices include data invaluable to the Corvette enthusiast: statistics of sales, options, colors and production; specification tables of engines and chassis, with serial number sequences and engine and option identification codes; a listing of Corvette clubs and a bibliography for further reading.

Corvette: America's Star-Spangled Sports Car is a book for anyone who ever drove a Corvette — or wanted to. It takes you behind the curtain of corporate secrecy with details, drawings and photos of many never-before-seen experimental cars, prototypes and styling studies. You meet men like Ed Cole, Bunkie Knudsen, John DeLorean and stylist Bill Mitchell as you learn all about the great sports car they wanted to build — and did. It's quite a story.

SIMPLY WRITE IN "CADILLAC BOOK" AND/OR "CORVETTE BOOK" ON THE INSIDE OF THE ENVELOPE.

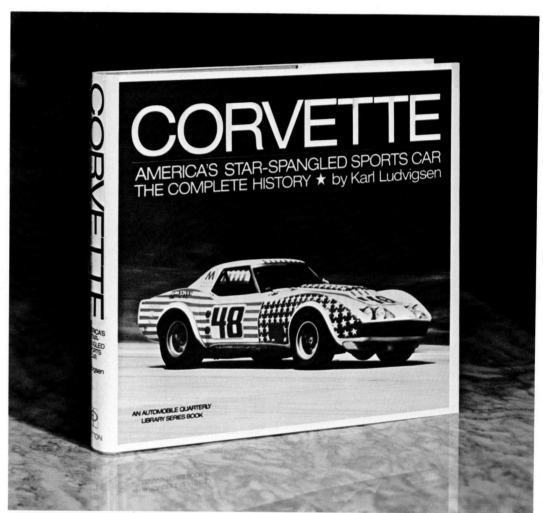

8½ x 9½ INCHES • APPROXIMATELY 300 PAGES
MORE THAN 300 PHOTOGRAPHS
A PORTFOLIO OF 50 EXPERIMENTAL, PRODUCTION AND RACING CORVETTES—IN FULL COLOR
REGULAR PRICE: $16.95   PRICE TO AQ SUBSCRIBERS: $14.95

Notes & Photo Credits

FRANK ROWSOME, JR. is the author of *The Verse by the Side of the Road,* a delightful book devoted to the Burma-Shave phenomenon. It prints the texts of all the jingles that were ever used—plus a few that couldn't be. An amateur student of auto-related advertising, he has also written a small book about Volkswagen ads, inevitably titled *Think Small*—and another one, *They Laughed When I Sat Down,* an informal history of magazine advertising. It covers a number of classic automotive ads such as "The Penalty of Leadership" for Cadillac and "Somewhere West of Laramie" for the Jordan Playboy. Mr. Rowsome's daytime typewriter marches to a very different drummer; he is chief of scientific and technical publications for NASA.

ANTHONY PRITCHARD, born in London in 1939, is a lawyer by profession and a writer by inclination. He has a specialist interest in competition cars of the Fifties, an interest stemming from days spent at Silverstone as a schoolboy at a time when British power in motor racing was just beginning to grow through the support of wealthy amateurs —and the dearest wish of every British enthusiast was to see a British Racing Green Grand Prix car defeat the red of Ferrari and Maserati. Books authored by him include *British Racing Green,* which is devoted to the aspirations of British constructors in the postwar years; a racing history of Porsche; and *The Racing Sports Car.* His latest book, *Grand Prix Ferrari,* is being published in London and New York this fall. He also writes an annual review of motor sport, *The Motor Racing Year.* Mr. Pritchard is nowadays a keen Porsche enthusiast and attends many of the major European races at the wheel of his 911. His interests extend well beyond motor racing, and he is at present researching for a biography of Cardinal Mazarin.

COVER
Illustration by Tom Fornander.

CONTENTS PAGE
The Commander Starlight from 1950 is owned by George W. Mills. Photograph by Rick Lenz.

STUDEBAKER
230 above left, 236 above right and below left: Courtesy of E. T. Reynolds. 230 above center, 230 below right, 231 above, 232 left center: Courtesy of Howard Applegate. 230 below left, 232 below center, 235 above left and right, 235 below left, 246 above right: Courtesy of the Corporate Records of Studebaker Automotive Division, at Syracuse University. 232 above right, 233 below left, 233 right, 237 above and below, 238 above and below, 241 above and below, 244-245 above center, 245 above right, 246 below left, 248 above and below, 252 above right, 253 below, 256 below left and right: Photographs by Rick Lenz. 233 above left: Photograph by Henry Austin Clark, Jr. 234 above, 239 above left, 244-245 below center, 246 above left, 247 above, 252 below, 253 above, 254-255 above center, 255 above right, 256 above: Photographs by Richard M. Langworth. 239 above right, 239 below, 240 below, 242-243, 247 below, 249 above and below, 250-251, 252 above left: Photographs by Don Vorderman. 240 above: Photograph by Russ Berry. 245 below right: Photograph by William Jackson. 254-255 below center: Photograph by the Grand Touring Auto Club (Carbondale). The editors wish to thank Howard T. Applegate, George E. Domer, Ed Flaherty, Asa Hall, Herb Keller, Otto Klausmeyer, Henry Muller, Marv Silverstein and Bruce Slifer for their assistance in research; Fred K. Fox, who kindly read the preliminary manuscript; Lloyd Taylor, director of the Studebaker Historical Collection in South Bend; Linda Lange, Jim Kile and other members of the Michiana Chapter of the Studebaker Drivers Club for their assistance in our photography sessions at the 1971 S.D.C. national convention. Antique Studebaker Club, 175 May Avenue, Monrovia, California 91016. Studebaker Drivers Club, Box 3044, South Bend, Indiana 46619. Studebaker Owners Club, Box 5294, Pasadena, California 91107.

STUDEBAKER AS GLADIATOR
260-261 above center, 261 above right: Courtesy of the Automotive History Collection, Detroit Public Library. 260-261 below center: Courtesy of Howard Applegate. 262 below, 263 above and below: Courtesy of E. T. Reynolds. All other photographs courtesy of the author. The author wishes to thank E. T. Reynolds for reviewing the manuscript and permission to quote certain remarks by Mr. Reynolds in previous accounts. Thanks also to the STP Corporation and Studebaker-Worthington, Inc.

THE STARLIGHT AND THE STARLINER
268 below, 270 left above, 271-272 below center, 271 above right: Courtesy of Holden Koto. 268 above, 269 below left and right, 270 above right, 271 below right: Courtesy of the Corporate Records of Studebaker Automotive Division, at Syracuse University. 269 above right, 272 above right: Courtesy of Howard T. Applegate Collection. 272 below right, 273 below: Courtesy of Robert F. Andrews. All other photographs courtesy of the author or from the files of AUTOMOBILE *Quarterly.* Sincere appreciation for their assistance in research to Robert F. Andrews, John W. Ebstein, Holden Koto and Raymond Loewy.

STUDEBAKER TODAY
Photographs by Don Vorderman.

AVANTI II
Photographs by Don Vorderman. We are grateful to Arnold Altman, vice-president, Avanti Motor Corporation, for the use of his personal Avanti II during preparation of this article. Thanks also for his superb hospitality and good fellowship to Nathan D. Altman, Avanti Motors president. Avanti Owners Association, Box 2626, Cincinnati, Ohio 45201.

BUGATTI TYPE 41, LA ROYALE
282-283: Photograph by Don Vorderman. The author wishes to express his gratitude to Miles Coverdale, and Jim Edwards of Harrah's Automobile Collection for their invaluable counsel in the preparation of this article. Bugatti Owners Club, 40 Bartholomew Street, Newbury, Berkshire, England, American Bugatti Club, 140 East 37th Street, New York, New York 10016. Bugatti Club de France, c/ Francois Ferdinand, 2 & 4 Pont Villars ,Valenciennes, 59 Nord, France. Registro Bugatti Italiano, Via Campo Sportivo 5, 36015 Schio, Italy.

BUGATTI ROYALE IMPRESSIONS
Photographs by Don Vorderman.

BURMA-SHAVE
Photographs courtesy of Burdette Booth and Allen Odell. Thanks for his assistance in research and photographic quests to John R. Olson.

CONNAUGHT
318-319, 320-321, 322-323: Courtesy of Guy Griffiths Motofoto. 324 above and center, 326 center and below, 327 below: Courtesy of *Autocar* magazine. 324 below: Courtesy of T. C. March. 327 center: Courtesy of Keystone Press Agency Ltd.

AL10: STILL RUNNING—AND WINNING
Photographs by Don Vorderman.

The Connaught emblem is debossed on the back cover.

... HOW TO ORDER PRINTS FROM THIS ISSUE ...

Full-size color prints with white borders, suitable for framing, are available of selected paintings, drawings and color photographs appearing in every issue of AUTOMOBILE *Quarterly.* Prints are priced according to their size: single page, one dollar fifty; one and a half page, one dollar seventy-five; double page, two dollars, foldouts, three dollars. Prices of portfolios vary according to size and number of paintings. The prints available from this issue are listed by page number. To order, please use the postpaid envelope enclosed.

AVANTI II: pages 280-281

BUGATTI: pages 298-299
pages 302-303
Royale paintings by Ted Lodigensky,
portfolio of six, ten dollars

CONNAUGHT: pages 330-331
cutaway drawings, pages 332-333

STUDEBAKER: pages 232, 233, 234
pages 237, 238, 239
pages 240, 241
pages 242-243
pages 244-245
pages 246, 247, 248, 249
pages 250-251
pages 252, 253
pages 254-255
page 256